Diary of a Taxi Driver

True stories from Singapore's most educated cabdriver

Cai Mingjie, PhD

Aktive Learning
10 Anson Road #21-02
International Plaza
Singapore 079903

E-mail: publisher@aktive.com.sg
Online book store: http://www.aktive.com.sg
Book website: http://www.diaryofataxidriver.com

ISBN 978-981-08-5020-3

National Library Board Singapore Cataloguing in Publication Data

Cai, Mingjie, 1953-
        Diary of a taxi driver : true stories from Singapore's most
educated cabdriver / Cai Mingjie. – Singapore : Aktive Learning,
c2010.
        p. cm.
        ISBN-13 : 978-981-08-5020-3 (pbk.)

        1. Cai, Mingjie, 1953- – Blogs. 2. Taxicab drivers – Singapore
– Blogs. 3. Taxicab drivers – Singapore – Diaries. I. Title.

HD8039.T162
388.413214092 -- dc22   OCN500934708

Printed in Singapore

Contents

Preface

It was a remarkable process to transition from a career scientist and professor to a taxi driver.

I had been a Principal Investigator (PI) at Singapore's leading molecular and cell biology research institute since 1992. After new management arrived a few years ago, a number of laboratories were shut down and mine was among the first to go. My employment contract with the institute was terminated in May 2008.

Initially, I found it difficult to accept my termination as it defied all my deeply rooted beliefs – I was expecting to be promoted instead of fired! When we were first enticed to set up laboratories in the then newly established research institute in the early nineties, Singapore was still unknown in the world of the biological sciences. It was through a decade of hard work by all the researchers and support staff of the institute that we were able to achieve world-class status in molecular and cellular biological research.

I have contributed my share to this development. My lab was recognized internationally in the research field of actin and endocytosis. We pioneered a number of important discoveries and made a significant contribution, especially in the aspect of regulation by phosphorylation (you can read more about my research in the appendix of this book).

Along with the scientific achievements, my lab also became one of the most productive in student training, generating the quantity and the quality of PhD scientists that I was, and still am, most proud of. Furthermore, as the chairman of the Graduate Admission Committee of the institute for nearly ten years, I and my fellow colleagues on the Committee were responsible for recruiting all the students of the institute during this period of time. These students had proved to be the major work force behind the scientific accomplishments that made the institute what it is today. I was also regularly invited to participate in the selection process of some prestigious national scholarships. Despite my sixteen years of dedication, I found myself out of job at the height of my career.

Becoming jobless at my age is perhaps the worst nightmare for any ordinary man. Unlike some colleagues of mine who had been similarly dismissed from the institute but since obtained academic positions in other countries, I could not leave because of my family. Since May 2007 when I was informed that my employment contract would not be renewed, I tried hard to find a job in Singapore. I submitted numerous CVs and application letters to various organizations including universities, government agencies, and private companies.

A university I had been associated with for many years as an adjunct faculty member was unenthusiastic about my application and never gave me a clear answer. Another university at first showed considerable interest and offered me a position of tenured professorship, but mysteriously did not follow through in the end. Most of the other organizations did not respond to my letters or emails. The few places I did receive an initial response from either gave me a straightforward rejection or were never heard from again. Later, the outbreak of the global financial crisis extinguished any hope I had left of finding a commensurate job. By November 2008, I finally made a decision to become a taxi driver.

In times of economic crises, the taxi business is one of the few that still actively recruits people. I signed up for a training course run by a government-linked transport company in November 2008, paying a course fee of nearly

$280. On paper, the Express Taxi Driver's Vocational License Course (or TDVL) is supposed to run six days a week, five hours a day. But in reality the course never lasted longer than three hours. It was divided into five sections: rules and regulations, routes and landmarks, names and locations of buildings, defensive driving, and the general paper (which included subjects such as highway codes, vehicle maintenance, healthy living and so on). The instructors were either veteran taxi drivers or representatives from government agencies.

My class started on the 1st of December, 2008, consisting of more than thirty people. There were three classes running at the same time and all were about this size. The lessons were easy. Every day, the instructors drew attention to certain parts in the manual and asked us to memorize them because they would be tested. As long as you could regurgitate that, it was impossible to fail the test. Even if you failed, you still had one year to take an unlimited number of retests. With such ease it is unsurprising that there are nearly 100,000 people who possess a taxi driver's license in Singapore today, almost three for every hundred citizens.

By the end of February 2009 I received my taxi driver's license, and began my new career. This book originated from a blog (http://taxidiary.blogspot.com/) I created to record the stories I experienced during my six month contract period with a taxi operating company as a hirer. They are all actual events and were first recorded as notes I scribbled down between fares, then later written up as truthfully as I could remember. I have taken precautions to avoid revealing any specific information which may be used to identify any person described within (with one or two exceptions).

My aim is to give my readers a firsthand account of life as a rookie taxi driver in Singapore. While the views and encounters described in this work may be trivial, I hope my readers will find these real life stories interesting and helpful in widening their perspectives.

Finally, I want to thank my family for their trust and support, and for always being at my side through the distress and anxiety of my job loss. I also want to thank all my customers, especially the ones who have shown their grace, kindness, and understanding to me when I made mistakes during my work. They gave me the motivation to carry on.

Day One

Today I collected my taxi, a Toyota Crown. The taxi company splits this model into two categories: one to three years old, and three to five years old. The former costs $93 per day to rent, the latter $77. I went for the cheaper one.

Even with the cheaper rental, I knew it was going to be hard for me to earn a living. Every day I hear news of the economy being in bad shape. I have seen long lines of empty taxis waiting for customers at various taxi stands. The official data on taxi ridership has shown a drastic drop in recent times. But I am determined to give it a try.

My three-year-and-nine-month old taxi had 346,800 kilometers of mileage on it, equivalent to more than thirty years normal usage of a family car in Singapore. It looked worn beyond its age, and was noisy and cumbersome to drive.

After I drove out of the company's taxi depot, I stopped at the side of a small, deserted road and wondered where to go. I sat there and stared at the barren space that surrounded me. In my heart, I felt daunted by the prospect of picking up passengers off the roads, as I was far from ready to provide a service to them. My knowledge of roads and buildings was still woefully inadequate. In my head, however, I knew clearly that there was no room for hesitation now. "开弓没有回头箭" (the extended bow has no choice but to fire the arrow), as the Chinese saying goes. Finally, I took a deep breath, restarted the car, and said to myself, "Today is the day. Let's do it."

I drove straight to the city.

From the taxi stand of the Outram Park MRT train station, I picked up my first customer. I was greatly relieved to hear him say that he wanted to go to the Tan Boon Liat building. This building is one of the landmarks tested in the taxi driver's license test and I knew exactly where it was even though I had never been there. It was just a short distance away from the taxi stand.

The customer told me he was from the Philippines and asked if I knew about a camera shop located in Tan Boon Liat. I said I was a new taxi driver and didn't have much knowledge about this place. He said never mind then.

As we were close to the building, I realized a problem. The Tan Boon Liat building is located on a block surrounded by four one-way streets, and I didn't know where the entrance was. I hit the Holiday Inn Hotel next door before turning around to finally end up at the main gate of the building. The meter fare was $4.60. I offered to take $3.60.

But the man said, "It's okay. It's your time too." He paid the fare in full.

It was a good start because my first customer was a kind one. My next three passengers all knew their way and guided me to their destinations without any incident.

By 6pm, I decided I had enough stress for the day and joined my family for dinner. My wife has always been supportive of me, but I was worried about my eight year old son. I didn't tell him I had lost my job, and no longer worked in that nice office he used to visit and play computer games in (before the new management of the institute barred the entry of all children into the building for safety reasons). He didn't know I was going to be a taxi driver. I was unsure how he would react to the sudden change of his dad's occupation.

I was delighted that he didn't mind at all when he saw me driving an old taxi home. I knew he was still too young to fully understand what had happened to me, but as long as he is happy, I will be happy too. That is all I care about.

Broken Barrier and Two Unforgettable Customers

(1)

My first passenger today was a young man who boarded my taxi near the Pan Pacific Hotel. He told me to go to Jurong via the AYE.

When we reached his condominium entrance, there was a van stopped at the gate and a guard was taking down its plate number. After the van went in, I drove closer to the guard and stopped. My passenger, let's call him Mr. L, raised his hand to the guard, a dark skinned lady, who recognized him and waved her hand to motion me to enter. As I proceeded, the gate barrier that had been up after the van entered suddenly dropped. The barrier was bent by an advertisement structure mounted on the roof of my taxi. The guard called the estate manager and a woman in her mid twenties came out of the management office. Mr. L, who had settled the fare with me and left, came back when he saw the manager coming.

"Don't worry," he said to me, "it's not your fault. I will be your witness."

As the lady manager was briefed by the guard, Mr.

L and I approached them and Mr. L started to tell the girl that the taxi proceeded upon the guard's permission and therefore was not responsible for what happened. The manager didn't pay much attention to him. She went into the guardhouse and looked at the video recording of the incident. We followed her and watched the video together.

After viewing the whole thing, she turned to me and said, "I can't see the guard waving her hand to you from the video. You or your company must pay for the damage. The incident was totally your fault."

I couldn't see the guard waving her hand from the video either. The camera was placed at such an angle that most of the image of the guard was blocked by my taxi.

The girl then said to me, "Which company are you working for? Do you have a valid license? Show me."

I gave her my license and she took down my details. Meanwhile, Mr. L, annoyed by the girl's ignoring of him, protested loudly that I was not to be blamed for the damage. He said the management should absorb the cost of the repair, rather than imposing it on the "poor" taxi driver.

The girl turned to me and asked, "You do have insurance from your company, don't you?"

"I don't know," I answered. "I am new. This is only my second day as a taxi driver."

I immediately regretted saying that.

The girl threw Mr. L a "you with me now?" sort of look.

An hour later I was finally allowed to leave. With the thoughts tumbling in my head about how much this incident would cost me, I felt totally exhausted.

In the past few days I hadn't been able to sleep well, only managing two or three hours a night. I needed to go home and take a nap.

At home, I first called the driver's assistance hotline of my company and reported the incident. The lady who took my call told me to report to the ARC (Accident Reporting Center) on Monday.

(2)

At four o'clock in the afternoon, I decided to go out again since I couldn't sleep no matter how hard I tried.

At Buangkok Hospital, a nurse-like young lady in her twenties boarded and said, "Uncle, can you take me to Sin Ming?"

I had no idea how to get to Sin Ming from Buangkok. I told the girl I was a new driver and apologized for not knowing the way. The girl was polite and gracious. She said she could understand how difficult and stressful it was to be a new taxi driver. Then she said, "I can probably direct you if you can take me to Upper Thomson."

I replied gladly, "Sure."

Upper Thomson Road is a major road and should be on every traffic signboard around the area. I was confident I would have no problem finding it.

As we were coming to the Upper Thomson Road junction, I asked the girl which way I should turn. She couldn't recognize any landmarks around the junction and was hesitant for a few seconds before saying, "Let's try the right hand side."

I continued on Upper Thomson Road after making the turn, but after a while the girl realized we were going the wrong way and asked me to make a U-turn.

When I finally reached her destination, the fare was over $10, much more than if I had taken the right route. I apologized again and offered to take $6. The girl paid in full and said to me before she left, "It's okay, uncle. Don't worry about it."

I felt deeply indebted to her, not for the $4 discount that she didn't take, but for her kindness and understanding. She could have taken another taxi at Buangkok when I told her I didn't know the way. There were at least three taxis behind me then, but she gave me a chance to learn.

This is how the little things you do in your daily life will impact the lives of others, without you knowing it.

The Singapore Army of Taxis

It was raining heavily in the afternoon, which is supposedly good for the taxi business, but I didn't benefit much from the rain. I did manage to ferry several passengers but the earnings were small as they were all short distances. By dinner time I had still not made enough to cover the daily rental.

I decided to try my luck at night and went out again at 11:30pm. I drove around for a long time without finding a single customer. Since the surcharge was fifty percent of the meter fare after midnight, it felt like every taxi in the city (the official figure puts it at more than 24,000) was out looking for business. The streets were full of empty taxis. They came like an army of bees, stopping at the red traffic lights, then racing each other as soon as the light turned green. Most of the time, they race for nothing. Occasionally there would be someone waiting down the road and that became the prize for the winning bee.

I didn't get anybody after two hours of cruising. Tired and disappointed, I decided to go home at 1:50am.

In the three days since I began driving, my total

earnings were just about enough to cover the rental, but not the fuel. And that is only because the first day, the taxi collection day, was rental free. I have to do better.

Mar 2009
2
Monday

Water Goes Lower, Man Goes Higher

(1)

My first task in the morning was to go to the company Accident Reporting Center. The whole bureaucratic procedure took more than three hours. The "center" was actually a tiny room, crowded with taxi drivers involved in accidents of one kind or another. I had to wait outside as there was no space inside to sit or even stand. When my turn finally came, I was given some forms to fill and questioned by an officer. I wrote down the details of the incident on one of the forms. I also told the officer that my passenger was willing to be my witness and defend me in this case. The officer asked if it was possible to get a statement from him and I said yes. Mr. L had given me his contact number. I was confident he would be willing to write a statement for me.

After lunch, I texted Mr. L and asked if he could write a statement for me and he immediately replied saying he would be glad to. I gave him my email address and he replied that he would do it right away.

(2)

Around midnight, at the entrance to a construction site of an HDB housing project, a young man in his late twenties flagged down my taxi and asked me in Mandarin to wait for him to bring some boxes. He filled the car with carton boxes and suitcases and told me to go to Geylang, Singapore's famous red light district. On the way I asked half-jokingly, "What do you need these boxes for in Geylang?"

He said he was moving to Geylang to stay with his friends for a while. Recognizing his accent, I asked where he was from. Sure enough, he was from my hometown in China. He told me he came to Singapore about a year ago as a foreign worker in the construction industry. He was leaving his current job at the construction site as he believed he could find another one with better pay. I asked, "How much did they pay you over at the construction site?"

"$50 a day."

"My friend," I sighed, "that's already more than I can make with this wheel."

And he replied with a Chinese proverb: "人往高处走，水往低处流" (water goes lower, man goes higher.)

After he left, I thought about what "man goes higher" meant. For most people it would mean higher pay, higher education, higher social status, a higher position on the food chain. That would be the normal course of a man's life. My transformation from a scientist and professor to a taxi driver would surely qualify for a classic example of the exact opposite of "man goes higher". But I look at it differently. Yes, the people sitting high on the food chain can make me jobless. What it has done to me, however, is only to push me to a "new high", a new boundary where I don't have to survive by playing *their* games. Low or high, I can take it either way. In fact, I am happier now as a taxi driver than in my last two years as a professor, when I often had to feel sorry for myself for having to work in that environment.

I turned on the radio. One of my favorite singers, Michael Buble, was singing *Feeling Good*. I hummed along on my way home.

Breakeven Point

Today was my longest driving day so far. I went out in the morning around 9:30am and came back at night around 2:30am. I finally made some profit.

I estimated that on an average driving day I need to make about $110 to break even, i.e. to cover the fuel and rental. Today I earned $170 in total or $60 in profit. I was happy with that.

Mar 2009

4

Wednesday

An Unlucky Day

(1)

Today was my unlucky day.

In the morning, I was called to report to the Accident Reporting Center. There, I was shown a video recording the ARC officer had acquired from the condominium where I damaged the gate barrier. The video was the same one I had seen before. It didn't show the guard giving me permission to enter as she was blocked by my taxi. It did show, however, that my taxi proceeded even after the barrier dropped down on the roof of the car (there was no way I could see the barrier dropping from my position). It was clear that the video was not in my favor. The ARC officer told me it was likely I had to pay for the damage, which was estimated to be $550. According to the company's insurance policy, drivers have to dish out the first $900.

"What about the witness?" I asked. I had submitted the witness statement from Mr. L to the ARC office a couple days ago.

"The witness statement is indeed strongly in your defense. But I am afraid it will not be worth much if they use this video as evidence," the officer replied. "Besides, they could argue that even if the guard waved her hand, she could just be saying hello to the passenger."

"Ok, that's fine. I will pay for it." With that, I stood up and left.

(2)

In the afternoon, I took a middle-aged lady from Ang Mo Kio to Centerpoint on Orchard Road, going by the CTE. There are two exit points to Orchard Road on the CTE. The first is Cairnhill Circle, followed shortly by Orchard Road. I knew that Cairnhill Circle was the exit I should take, but I wanted to make sure. By looking at her in the rear view mirror, I had deemed this poker-faced lady as someone who was unlikely to tolerate the slightest mistake. I asked her, "Should I take the Cairnhill Circle exit?"

Instead of giving me a direct answer, she said bluntly, "I told you I am going to Centerpoint," as if she had been bothered by something irrelevant.

That confused me momentarily and for some reason I took her response as a "no". That was a mistake.

As we were passing through the Orchard Road exit, the lady became furious, and shouted at me, "I told you I am going to Centerpoint, not Plaza Singapura! Why you take me here?"

I had no choice but to apologize as it was largely my fault. I said sorry I missed the right exit, and told her she could pay me whatever she wanted when we got there. In the end, the meter showed $13 plus an ERP charge of $1. The lady tossed a $10 note onto the front passenger seat and slammed the door as she got out.

(3)

The real disaster was yet to come.

During the evening rush hour, my taxi broke down in

the middle of a busy street in Chinatown. It just died on me when I stopped at a traffic light. I immediately called the driver assistance hotline. It took forty-five minutes for the tow truck to come. Meanwhile I had to stand in the middle of the road behind my dead taxi, redirecting the heavy evening traffic at the junction of New Bridge Road and Upper Pickering Road. Thousands of people passed by and looked down at me through the bus windows. I tried my best not to look back.

It was the longest forty-five minutes in my life.

As a result, today was a totally unproductive day.

Time Is Money

(1)

I often hear people say time is money. Now I really know it. Every minute of every day is measured in dollars and cents as far as my company is concerned. Every day they transfer $77.04 from my bank account, even if I am sick or unable to work for any reason. If my car is in the workshop for repair, the rental will be offset by "down time". The way the company calculates "down time", the rental divided by all the minutes in twenty-four hours, is really not fair to people like me who work a one man operation, because it disregards our rest time. But rest or no rest, sick or well, it is not their concern. The main thing they stressed repeatedly during our orientation was the importance of having sufficient funds in our bank account by midnight every day.

In the morning, I called the workshop to check on my taxi and was told it would be ready by lunch time. I didn't bother to ask how much "down time" they had granted to me. After I got the car back, I found that they had replaced the battery and something called "electric alternator carbon". The worksheet read: "Manufacturer recommended hours, 1.7, Actual activity hours, 59.4." This must be a good example of how far a company could go to save costs.

(2)

Five minutes before five in the afternoon, a middle-aged man boarded my taxi from a taxi stand along Shenton Way and told me to go to Yio Chu Kang. On the way, we had a pleasant conversation about a lot of things. It turned out he worked in a firm that handled certain public affairs for an institute where I knew many people as colleagues. At the end of the journey he paid $20 for the meter fare of just over $16.

"You know," he said after he got out the car, "most taxi drivers will wait till five to pick up passengers from there but you didn't."

I realized he had given me what I would have got if I had picked him up a few minutes later. In Singapore, taxi passengers leaving the CBD between 5pm and midnight have to pay a $3 surcharge. What a nice man!

Maybe he was also telling me not to be so naïve next time?

A Cabby Friend

An officer from the ARC called me this morning and told me he managed to reduce the cost of the barrier to $400. It was the best he could do, he said, and the money would have to be paid in person at the company as soon as possible. I thanked him and promised to come over to settle the matter soon.

One of my cabby friends from the training class called me in the afternoon, saying he was suspicious of his meter. He said he drove more than ten hours a day only to make twenty or thirty dollars after deducting the cost of rental and fuel. He thought his meter was wrong. After I found out he was driving the $92/day type of taxi, I advised him to change to my type. "You can save $15 a day on the rental," I said.

He asked some questions about the condition of my taxi and said he would talk to the company about it.

Mar 2009

7

Saturday

Leave The Boat Untied

In the afternoon, I took a Malay family (a mother, two teenage daughters and a little boy) from Upper Serangoon to Bedok Reservoir. I didn't know how to get there and neither did they, but the mother didn't seem too concerned about it.

"Just follow the bus and you will get there," she said blithely.

"Which bus?" I asked.

"Any bus," she laughed, apparently at herself.

I didn't have to follow any buses, not when I had a street directory with me. I checked the map and found the best route.

On the way, the mother and her daughters were talking in Malay. They talked and laughed, laughed and talked, for the whole journey. Nothing in this world seemed to be able to spoil their high spirits.

I didn't know what they were saying or laughing about, but as I was driving, a poem by Shu Sikong of the Tang dynasty came to mind:

钓罢归来不系船，
江村月落正堪眠。
纵然一夜风吹去，
只在芦花浅水边。

The moon is falling and village sleeping,
Go home, leave the boat untied.
The night wind may come and send it drifting,
You'll still find it close, along the shallow side.

Pardon my amateur translation, but the idea is there.
And that's the spirit I like.

Mar 2009

8

Sunday

The Customer Chain

In the morning, I drove a lady with several grocery shopping bags from Toa Payoh to a condominium in Lorong Chuan. After she left, I discovered that leaks from her bags had made my car floor wet and smelly. I had to spend a whole hour washing and drying the floor mats. I was really annoyed.

The taxi business is a mysterious thing. Sometimes you drive around for a long time without a single passenger. Sometimes one passenger leads to another and then again to another, like a chain linked together. This is of course purely fortuitous, but it makes you feel lucky when it happens.

Today, for instance, I got into a chain of five passengers starting from the lady who made me wash my taxi for an hour. After the wash, I got flagged down by a white lady at the exit gate of that same condo. She brought me to Holland Road, where a Japanese father and his daughter boarded as the lady got out. They were going to a golf game at the Tanah Merah Country Club, where I picked up another passenger to go to River Valley, where someone boarded to go to Raffles Place. I had already started to forgive the lady on the way back from the Tanah Merah Country Club.

My Last Paper

My wife is going on a business trip today. She will not be back till Friday, which means I have to stay home at night to take care of my son.

In the afternoon, I took a white man in his fifties from the city to Jurong. As this was during peak hour, the traffic was slow. The man works for Exxon Mobil. He said his company has a big operation on Jurong Island, employing more than 10,000 people, mostly Singaporeans. This is probably one reason why the Singapore government treats foreign investors so well.

Stayed at home after 8pm. While my son was doing his homework, I read the page proofs of my research paper *Regulation of the yeast formin Bni1p by the actin-regulating kinase Prk1p*. After I lost my job, I still managed to publish three research papers, and this one would be the last. It was accepted for publication by *Traffic* a month ago. I received the page proofs yesterday, and must send it back first thing tomorrow.

A Malay Girl

I had very little sleep last night as I had to finish the proofreading of my paper. I felt very tired while driving on the streets in the morning. Several times I wanted to go back home to take a nap, but every time the idea was overruled. Since my wife was out of town and I couldn't come out to work during the night, I had to drive as much as possible during the day.

In the afternoon I picked up a Malay girl in her twenties from Chinatown to go to the HDB Hub in Toa Payoh. This was the first time I heard of the HDB Hub and I didn't know where it was. I asked the girl if she knew and she said she wasn't sure but could try to help me.

"If I can't help you," she said, "you can just drop me off somewhere in Toa Payoh and I will try to get to the place by myself."

That was the nicest thing I had ever heard from a passenger.

When we got to Toa Payoh (via the CTE), the girl was able to direct me to the Hub after all. As I expected, this was a business trip and she needed a receipt. However, there was an ERP charge of $1.50 that I didn't know how to include on the receipt. I was taught how to do it before at the company but I could never get my meter to work like I was told.

After two unsuccessful tries the girl said, "Never mind, uncle. I will just absorb it myself."

I felt terribly embarrassed as I gave her a receipt that was $1.50 short of what she paid.

After she left I said to myself, "I hope everyone could be like you, girl."

Another Would-Be Taxi Driver

(1)

In the morning at a bus stop near Bukit Merah, a man in his late forties flagged down my taxi. After he got in he showed me a piece of paper and said, "Uncle, can you take me to this place?"

I took a glance at the paper and smiled. I had one exactly like that. It was a notice from the Singapore Taxi Academy with information of schedules of the training courses along with a map indicating where the course was held. This man was following in my footsteps to become a taxi driver.

He looked tired. He told me he had been walking around for more than an hour looking for this place, and nobody seemed to know where it was. I said, "I do. I just spent three weeks there not long ago. It is just around the corner."

On the way I said jokingly, "If you can't read a map, how can you be a taxi driver?"

The man ignored that. He started to ask a lot of questions about the training course and how the taxi business was nowadays. "The business is so so," I replied. The man appeared a little disappointed.

(2)

After the evening peak hours, there were a lot of people inside the CBD waiting for taxis. They all waited for the peak hours to end so they didn't have to pay the 35% surcharge. I took an Indian man in his forties from Shenton Way to Whampoa. The final fare was $11, $8 on the meter plus a $3 CBD surcharge. The man first gave me $10 and then searched his pocket for a while and said, "Uncle, I am ten cents short. Is it ok?"

I said, "Of course, no problem."

So he gave me ninety cents in coins, while holding a $2 note between his fingers.

I thought about the Malay girl I met yesterday.

Mar 2009
13
Friday

An Indian Friend

(1)

It was raining heavily in the morning and I nearly had an accident at Collyer Quay. While I was trying to change lanes with my turning lights blinking, a bus zoomed past my side. I would surely have collided with it if I didn't instantly straighten my wheels. How could anybody drive a bus so fast in the rain when the visibility was so poor?

I have to be more careful. I know by now that I can't drive a taxi like I drive a family car, since it seems nobody gives way to taxis on the road.

(2)

I picked up an Indian man in his mid thirties from Outram to go to Bukit Batok around midnight. He spoke Chinese surprisingly well. We had an enjoyable conversation during the journey. At one point I said to him that I think in Singapore, taxi drivers are at the bottom of society. I, for example, work twelve, sometimes fifteen hours a day only to take home $30 to $50. I have no weekends and no holidays, and must work seven days a week the whole year round. If I am sick and unable to work for any reason, I still have to pay for the rental. The truth is, taxi drivers get paid a small amount of money by working harder than almost anybody else, and *pay other people money* if they don't work or don't work hard enough.

He thought about it for a moment and said, "Well, today is different. Today, something funny happens."

By then we had come to the end of the trip. He first paid the fare, which was $12.20, and then he drew out a $50 note and put it in my hand and said, "This is a tip." With that, he got out of the car.

I rushed out of the car and ran after him, "No, no, no. I can't take this."

At this moment, the taxi started to slide backwards on the street. It was parked along a sloping street and I had forgotten to pull up the hand break before I rushed out! I quickly put the money into his hand and rushed back to the car to stop it with the hand break. Luckily, there were no other cars on the street at this time of the night.

This stunt shocked him. With the $50 in his hand, he stood there in astonishment and said, "Okay, man, you scared the hell out of me."

I said, "No sweat. You take care, brother." With that, I drove off.

Working Girls

(1)

In the morning an anxious looking man with a cell phone pressed on his ear flagged down my taxi on Cross Street in Chinatown and told me to go to the Toa Payoh HDB Hub. "I am in a hurry," he added.

He was talking with somebody on the phone and begging for more time. "I am in a cab already. Just give me ten more minutes and I will be there. Please?"

I drove as fast as I could. Since the trip with the Malay girl, I had learned to get to the HDB Hub via the CTE. I got there in no time. The man got out of the car hurriedly with a thank you.

I hope I had helped him.

(2)

Packed lunch and ate at the Telok Blangah Hill Park. This place had become my favorite lunch site – this was the third time in a week I had come here to eat. I like it because it is cool, windy, and very quiet. Not many people come here. There is also a public washroom which is reasonably clean and has enough water coming out of the tap to let you really wash your hands.

I sat on the bench for a while after eating, watching my cigarette smoke dissolve into the peacefulness that surrounded me, before reluctantly heading back to the car.

(3)

After midnight a girl in her twenties boarded my taxi near Lorong 20, Geylang. She passed a cell phone to me after she got in. A man on the other end of the line, who sounded like a local, told me to take the girl to Eunos MRT. I said okay.

On the way, the girl started talking on the phone again, apparently with the same man.

"I don't want to go to your house. I want to go to a hotel."

She sounded like she was from one of the South East Asian countries. She repeated it one more time, a bit louder. Apparently failing to get an agreement from the man, she flipped her phone shut and said to me, "Uncle, turn back. I am going to Orchard now."

At the roadside on Orchard Boulevard, where the girl asked to be dropped off, two girls got in as the other girl got out. A strong, stomach-whirling smell of perfume came in with them. One said to me, "Orchard Tower."

It was a man's voice.

The Orchard Towers building is just a stone's throw from where they boarded. They could have walked there with the time spent waiting for a taxi. The streets are safe, even at this hour. Obviously, they didn't want to be seen by people on the streets. They were both men and talked with each other in normal men's voices. When we were near the Orchard Towers building one said to me, "Uncle, can you drive in a little further?" in a woman-like voice. Clearly, being near to his workplace had automatically activated his acting mode.

They were ready to start work.

And I was ready to go home. At the junction leading into my residence, a big white man and small Asian woman were kissing each other by the roadside, waiting for a taxi. They broke up when they saw me and stopped me. The white man wanted me to take the girl to Bedok. I recognized him but I don't think he recognized me. I said sorry I couldn't go that far. It was almost 3am.

Two White Men

(1)

In the evening, a white man in his fifties boarded my taxi from the west side of the city and told me to go to Geylang. On the way there he talked to me about career changes, after he guessed correctly that I was an academic turned taxi driver. He told me there were several times in his life when his career was interrupted and he was able to bounce back every time. Now he was a director of an internationally renowned academic institution. He told me to never give up on my dreams. I thanked him. I thought it was very nice of him to offer such heartfelt encouragement to a stranger.

Amidst our conversation, he didn't forget to say that he was not going to Geylang to get laid, obviously trying to protect his image after he told me who he was. While a bit taken aback by his directness, I thought best to let that statement slip without reply.

(2)

After midnight a white man in his forties boarded my taxi from the Orchard Towers taxi stand. He called somebody and started talking wildly, apparently about his sexual experience moments ago. He thanked the person for introducing two girls to him. He was clearly very satisfied with them. He excitedly shouted about his encounters to the other person as if I was not present.

Of course, who cares about taxi drivers?

An Angry Old Man

In the morning, outside the Tongji Hospital, a man in his seventies and a lady in her thirties boarded my taxi and said in Mandarin to go to the market in Chinatown.

"Which market?" I asked.

"You are not a Singaporean!" All of a sudden, the old man poured a stream of angry words onto me. "You are a Chinese. How can you drive a taxi? Do you have a taxi license? You don't know *Niu Che Shui* (Chinatown)? Many hundreds of years old, you don't know?"

I had no idea why the man was so angry, but I held my smile and said, "I just want to make sure where is it you want to go."

The lady was quick to come forward to defuse the situation, saying politely that it was the market opposite to People's Park.

It was still not specific enough. So I asked, "Is it the one behind Chinatown Point?"

"Yes," the lady replied.

However, as I was crossing New Bridge Road, the man again raged, "You should turn just now. Why you go this way?"

"I thought you said you are going to the market behind

35

Chinatown Point," I said.

It turned out they were going to the Smith Street Market. I said if they had told me it was the Smith Street Market in the beginning, it would have been no trouble at all. I may have problems with other parts of the city, but I do know Chinatown very well.

The meter fare was $4.40. I first told them that $4 would be fine, thinking it wasn't really my fault we had travelled some extra distance. The old man said, "You should just take three," while getting out.

"Okay, $3 would be just fine too," I said, refusing to let him spoil my day.

The lady said, "I'll give you $3.50." But she didn't have fifty cents. So she gave me $3.20 instead.

"Although Taxi Driver Is A Noble Job..."

This morning, a man boarded my taxi near Everton Park and told me to go to Novena Square.

"You must be new. How long have you been driving?" he asked, after making himself comfortable in the back seat.

"How do you know I am new?" I threw the question back, glad to oblige him.

"You wear long sleeves. Not many taxi drivers wear long sleeves. And you look very *si wen* (scholarly)." Then he added, "You must be a very handsome man when you were young."

"No, I am more handsome now than before," I said. "And yes, I am new. I only started driving about three weeks ago."

"What were you doing before?"

"I was a teacher."

"See, I knew it."

After he learned how I lost my job, he expressed his sympathy and said to me that it was not my disgrace to lose my job; it was the system's. Then he said, "Although taxi driving is a noble job…"

"A noble job?" I interrupted him. "You are the first person who said this to me."

"Yes, it is a noble job," he said. "A taxi driver has freedom. He is his own boss. And he charges his fees by the meter. Children or elderlies, men or women, all treated the same. But," he stressed, "but you ought to find a way to go back to your expertise. Many people can drive taxis, but not many can do what you did in your expert field. It is a terrible waste for you to drive a taxi."

I explained to him how difficult it was to find an academic position in a small place like Singapore. If I wanted to continue doing research I had to leave the country, which was something I couldn't do for family reasons. Nevertheless, I was still trying to make the best of the sorry situation. I told him I would use this experience to show myself and other people how to go on with life when extreme adversity strikes.

In the end, he paid $10 for a fare of just over $7.

He was over seventy years old. He used to own several factories in Singapore and Malaysia. He also invested in China many years ago but the business didn't work out as he was cheated by some people there. But that unpleasant experience did not affect his admiration for China and the Chinese people. He had insightful views about many things. He was a wise man.

Mar 2009
20
Friday

A Sad Man And A Hundred Dollars

(1)

I had lunch in a food court near Outram Park today. As I was having a post-meal cigarette, a man in his fifties came by and asked something in a dialect I couldn't understand. I asked if he could speak Mandarin and he said in Mandarin that he was dying for a cigarette and asked if I could spare one. I said sure. I gave him the pack. There was only one left in it. He said sorry to take the last one from me and I said no problem.

He took the cigarette, lit it, crouched on some stairs nearby and started smoking. I said to him, "Come sit here." He came over and sat on the chair across from me. His eyes avoided mine. After a while he looked up at the cloudy sky and said in a muted voice, "It's going to rain again."

He was dressed in a blue shirt and black long pants. The colors had partially faded with wash and wear, but the overall outfit looked neat and clean. And there was something in his appearance that suggested sophistication and intellect.

At first I thought maybe I could get him to tell me

something about himself. I was certain the man had quite a story to tell. But after I studied his face, I thought better of it.

I finished my cigarette, stood up, nodded to him and left without a word.

That man was in no state to entertain my company. His eyes, his mouth, his whole face, seemed to be saying, "Just leave me alone, please."

(2)

I picked up an old white couple from Lau Pa Sat after midnight. They told me to take them to Swissotel. They said they had been walking for the whole day and were now so tired they couldn't walk anymore. I said, "No problem. I will take you to your doorsteps."

In the end the fare was over $8 including the surcharges. The old man gave me two $50 notes and said "thank you and keep the change" while getting out of the car. I immediately knew he had mistaken the $50 notes for the $5 ones and called after him, "Wait, you have given me too much."

The $50 and $5 notes of the Singapore currency are very similar to each other. They have similar colors and patterns. The only notable difference is the size. Realizing her husband had made a mistake, the wife took back the hundred dollars and gave me $10 instead. She thanked me and left.

Men's Generosity

(1)

In the morning, I took a white man in his thirties from Commonwealth to the airport. He was from Australia and had been living and working here for some years. He said he liked Singapore, except it was too expensive, way too expensive compared with Australia, but he had to stay because of his job. He was in a very specialized industry and outside of it, he was simply unemployable.

"If I lose my job, I really don't know what else I can do," he said in a somewhat worried tone, as if he was talking about a real, rather than hypothetical, possibility.

I could surely sympathize with that. I told him I was in the same situation and had already become unemployable. That was how I became a taxi driver. But I am not just another taxi driver. I said I had a blog about taxi driving, and wanted to make it more interesting than people generally thought. He liked the idea and said he was looking forward to reading my blog.

(2)

In the late evening, two young men boarded my taxi in the financial district and asked to be taken to a KTV on

Shenton Way. They said they were told this was a famous KTV in Singapore and had walked a long way trying to find it. They sounded new to the town. I told them I knew a place on Shenton Way which might be the KTV they were looking for. "If it is not, you guys don't have to pay me," I said.

When we reached there after a short drive, they were greatly delighted. "Yes," they said, "this is the one."

"Then you need to pay now," I laughed.

"We are glad to."

They gave me $10 for a meter fare of $3.40 plus the $3 CBD surcharge.

(3)

I am beginning to get an idea of how big the population of Chinese prostitutes is in Singapore. Three times tonight I drove local Singaporean men romancing with ladies from China, all of whom spoke northern Chinese accents. Their conversations indicated they were probably underground prostitutes. Two pairs went to hotels. The last pair went to an HDB block in Ang Mo Kio. The man told the lady his wife was not at home because she had to attend some activities organized by her company. Some watchful neighborhood.

Two Youngsters

I felt very sick this morning. I had a sore throat that started yesterday afternoon. I took some Panadol before going to bed last night, but it didn't prevent my discomfort from getting worse today. I might have had a fever too but didn't check.

Still, I went out to do some business. I had to at least make enough money to cover the rental.

Past midnight, two young men boarded my taxi from Ang Mo Kio and said to go to Geylang. They were both teenagers. They were going to visit a brothel on Lorong 18. One of them was more experienced than the other. He was telling the other boy what to say to the girl to get started. He himself was going to see a girl he knew by a nickname; he seemed to know her very well.

I don't know if there is a legal minimum age to visit prostitutes in Singapore, like for drinking or smoking. If there is, these boys were surely underaged. I also wondered if their parents knew or cared about what their young boys were doing on the streets at this hour.

A Monk And Ms. Y

(1)

Sent my son to his grandma's place around ten in the morning. I had planned to return home to rest more, but a Buddhist monk in a scarlet robe appeared in front of me when I dropped my son off. He wanted to hire my taxi. So I let him in. He showed me a small folded piece of paper. On one side of the crease, it had "Tiong Bahru" handwritten on it, and on the other side, "851". He pointed to the paper and said in Mandarin that he wanted to go there.

On the way, I asked him where he was from. He said, "China."

"Where in China?"

"Beijing."

I was surprised. "But you don't have any Beijing accent."

"Oh," he searched for words for a moment. "Because I left home when I was very little."

His Mandarin was actually very poor. He not only didn't have a Beijing accent, but spoke like a foreigner just beginning to learn the language. His sentences were mostly broken and his pronunciation reminiscent of monks narrating Buddhist verses. Nevertheless, I managed to learn that he was sent to a Buddhist monastery (出家) when he was five, and had not seen his parents since. He was thirty-eight now. He belonged to the Dalai Lama school of Hindu Buddhism. He had been stationed in Taiwan for many years. He came to Singapore about two months ago, and would go back to Taiwan next month.

In Singapore, he stayed in Yishun. He spoke a little Mandarin and no English. The only way he knew how to get back to his place in Yishun was to take bus 851 from Tiong Bahru.

"I cannot go to China now," he said emotionlessly. "I cannot get a visa."

I wondered if he had any special desire to go to China, to see his parents, or to do a Buddhism exchange program like what he said he was doing in Singapore. I didn't ask. Neither did I tell him that if he wanted to enrich his knowledge of Buddhism, he should forget about visiting China. To my knowledge, temples and monasteries in China, like everything else there, have more to do with money than with religion now…unlike him.

He must be a true monk, I thought. A monk who had spent so much of his life reading the sutra that he even forgot how to speak his own native language.

The trip was short and the meter fare was $5. Just as I wondered if he had any money, he took out a wallet and started to look into it. I quickly said, "No money needed."

He looked at me with raised eyebrows, "Are you sure?"

"Yes," I replied, "I am sure. The ride is free."

He put away his wallet, said thank you, and got out.

(2)

After ferrying the monk, I came back home and slept till 4pm.

Went out again to catch the peak hour business. On Shenton Way a white lady who looked to be in her early forties boarded my taxi and said to go to Pasir Ris. I drove nervously on the way because Pasir Ris is one of the towns I was unfamiliar with. Sure enough, I missed the exit on the highway when we were near Pasir Ris. Instead of being upset, the lady, let's call her Ms. Y, remained very nice to me and patiently directed me to her place via a detour route.

This was how Ms. Y came to know that I was a new taxi driver and had recently lost my job as a researcher. After I told her I had been unable to find any job related to my education for more than a year, she asked what kind of credentials I had.

My credentials are solid gold, only their current market value in Singapore is less than a cent, I thought to myself.

After a moment's pause, I said, "I have a PhD from Stanford."

"What?" she almost jumped up. "I must give you my card." She quickly took out her business cards, gave one to me and said, "Write to my email listed on the card. And send your CV as well. I will see if I can help you find a teaching job."

The card said she worked for an American educational institution in Singapore. I thanked her and promised to write to her later.

(3)

The rest of the day was bad for me. My taxi is at a big disadvantage when it comes to competing with other taxis. Mine is just too slow. Today alone, I lost three customers to other taxis which overtook me from behind when they saw a customer. The new Hyundai Sonatas from Comfort and Citicab are especially fast. For more than three hours before and after midnight, I couldn't get a single job.

The Reality Of The Taxi Business In Singapore

My cabbie friend who called the other day about the meter called again today, and told me he was going to switch to the $77 rental taxi. He also said he was thinking about quitting. But quitting would cost him $300 in fines, and he had no other job to fall back on. I told him to hang on for a while, at least to see how the lower rental would pan out.

Again, the streets were full of taxis tonight. Most of them were running around empty.

According to the 2008 government figures, of the 894,682 motor vehicles in Singapore, 24,300 are taxis. And there were 92,535 valid taxi driver license holders at the end of 2007. I am sure it has since gone well over 100,000, or three in every 100 Singaporeans. I believe that may just be the highest percentage in the world.

You may wonder: if the demand is not there, why is there still an oversupply? The answer is that the taxi operating companies do not care about the demand in ridership. They only care about collecting rentals from the drivers. During an economic downturn, many people become jobless and they form an abundant source of potential taxi drivers. The taxi companies recruit these people, train them, give them the license, and get them to sign a taxi hiring contract for at least six months. In my case, if I quit within six months, I have to pay the company $300 for breach of contract. If I quit after six months, that is not a problem for the company either as they constantly run the "training course" to recruit new taxi drivers. The government figures say that new taxi driver licenses are given out at the rate of more than 5,000 a year.

This is the reality of Singapore's taxi industry today. The taxi operating companies do all they can to get every taxi rented out to drivers, regardless of the demand on the streets. As long as rentals are collected, they do not care how the drivers survive.

You can't blame them, though. All companies operate to seek maximum profit.

There is, however, something unique about the taxi business here. The taxi driver license can only be issued to Singapore citizens. I don't know of any other job in Singapore that has this requirement. Even strategically important agencies such as Temasek Holdings, which is responsible for safeguarding billions of dollars of Singapore's public wealth, do not require citizenship for their number one position. Therefore, either taxi driving is the most privileged job in Singapore, or it is the last resort to be reserved for Singaporeans when all other jobs shut them out.

The former is of course not true. It thus makes perfect sense that taxi driving is the hardest, most tedious and lowest paid job reserved exclusively for Singaporeans, as it is the last one available to them.

A Snob On The Road

(1)

I didn't know till today that you could identify a snob on the road. This afternoon when I was approaching a junction, I switched on my left turning light. A blue Lexus was at my rear on the extreme left lane. Instead of slowing down to let me filter in, it sped up just to close the gap between itself and the car in front, making it impossible for me to change lanes. As I continued signaling, the Lexus showed no sign it was going to give me a break.

At this time, a gorgeous red Mazda MX-5 convertible that had been in front of me for some time switched on its turning light: it was going to go left, too. This time, the Lexus slowed down good-naturedly and gave way to the convertible without delay.

My poor old Toyota Crown, with its turning light ticking tirelessly as if saying, "please, please, please…", waited for several cars to pass by until one finally let me in.

(2)

Late at night, around 1am, I picked up three ladies from Chinatown to go to Ang Mo Kio and Yishun. They were all in their late forties or early fifties. On the way, I asked why they had to work so late. The lady sitting beside me said jokingly that they do "very special work", while moving her hands around. I knew what she meant, massage. Then she started speaking in Hokkien, telling the other two about how she serviced some ang moh (Caucasian) guy. I could not understand Hokkien very well so I missed most of her story. But the story was surely amusing because the other ladies laughed their hearts out.

A Transvestite

(1)

In the morning around 11am, a white man in his forties and an elegantly dressed Asian woman in her early thirties boarded my taxi in front of a hotel on Bencoolen Street. Soon after the man said the name of a condo in the west, they got into a long moment of kissing. It was not until they started talking that I realized the woman was a man.

"I am flying out Sunday morning," the white man said.

"I want to see you again tomorrow," "she" said softly.

"We'll see," he said absently, "I will be busy tomorrow."

"You're free today, right?"

The man did not answer.

"Right?" "she" repeated.

"Yes, yes."

"I've been reading a book about gays' life." The "woman" started talking about a book "she" read recently. "She" liked the book very much and was eager to share "her" thoughts and what "she" learned from the book with the man. "She" seemed well-educated and well-read. The white man acknowledged "her" sporadically but didn't seem to be paying much attention.

When we reached the condo, it seemed that it was the white man whom the guard recognized before he motioned me to go in. But the "woman" also knew the place very well. "She" directed me to go to the basement carpark and told me where to turn and where to stop. So perhaps "she" was a regular visitor there.

Or perhaps not. I doubt any security guard in Singapore would bother to ask questions before opening the gate for a white stranger.

(2)

After 1am, a woman in her twenties flagged down my taxi on Havelock road. She asked me to take her to Tanah Merah prison. Before going there, she needed to stop at a 24-hour McDonald's to get something first. But I had no clue how to get to the prison, knowing only it was somewhere in a remote area of Upper Changi. I asked her and she didn't know either. Then I asked if she could give me a minute to allow me to check the street directory. She was hesitant to do so. She eyed the road where taxis with green lights on the top were passing by one after the other. I knew she was in a hurry and said, "It's okay. Go get another taxi."

On the way back home, I pondered what the lady might have been doing. She was unlikely a staff working in the prison, so she must be going there to visit somebody, who was probably hungry for a Big Mac.

But why at this hour?

A Young Couple

(1)

During my first month of taxi driving, I repeated the same mistake again and again – I always forgot to add the ERP and CBD surcharges to the fare. I have lost a lot of money this way. Today, for example, I forgot to charge the $3 CBD surcharge to a lady who took my taxi from Chinatown to the Singapore General Hospital. I had told her there would be a $3 surcharge on top of the meter fare before the trip started. But in the end I returned her change without including the CBD surcharge. The lady was hesitant for a second when she received the change, but didn't say anything before she left. I only remembered the surcharge a moment later after the lady was inside the building. I thought about going after her but abandoned the idea as soon as it came up.

(2)

I passed by Geylang several times today. One time, I took a young family with a small baby from there to Bukit Batok. As we crawled like a snail through the heavy traffic, the wife was playing with the baby in her arms.

"They don't look so pretty," she commented lightly, referring to the prostitutes standing along the street.

"The pretty ones are inside." The husband, who never took his eyes off the street since he got in, bit the bait. "They don't come out."

"Yah? How do you know?" she pursued. "Maybe you also know how much they cost?"

"Why?" He turned his head and looked at her. "You want to do that too if the money is good?"

"Why not? If the money is good." The lady looked up, holding his eyes as she answered.

"You think they are not pretty but you are worse than them," the husband said scornfully, his eyes returning to the street. "Nobody will want you…"

I listened and smiled. Sometimes the conversations of my customers are an entertainment to me and help me pass the tedious driving time. This was one of them.

First Warning

It was two in the morning. On my way home two ladies flagged down my taxi on Depot Road. The ladies told me to go Changi Airport Terminal Three. "The Arrival Hall, not the Departure Hall," one of them emphasized.

The area outside the Arrival Hall was deserted when we got there. No cars, no taxis, no people. Not a soul in sight. As I was getting the change for the ladies, someone tapped on my window. I looked up. Coming out of nowhere were two policemen, who motioned with a baton for me to lower my window. Politely and innocently, I held up one hand and said, "Hold on a second, let me finish this first," and went back to the money matters.

Three sharper, louder taps on my window immediately followed.

I stopped what I was doing and lowered the window.

"Who told you you can drop off your passengers here?" one of the policemen asked.

Now I realized I was in trouble. My mind started to race at once. I vaguely remembered that in our training class, the instructor from the LTA said something about dropping off and picking up passengers at the airport. Something off, something odd. But I couldn't recall what it was exactly.

"Er, my passengers asked me to drop them off here," I mumbled, while taking a quick look at the ladies, who by now had buried themselves behind the front seats, anxiously waiting for their change before they could escape from the crime scene.

"Do you listen to your passengers or to traffic police?" the policeman said with a superior grin. "Give me your license."

After he took a look at my license, he lifted his head obliquely, like a third grade teacher reacting to a simple mistake in his student's homework that he had corrected many times before. "A new driver," he sighed.

I began to let out the breath I had been holding the whole time.

"Okay, this is your lucky day," the policeman said. "We will give you a warning only this time. But next time you do this again, we will book you."

He took down my taxi plate number and my license number before he returned it to me and let me go.

On the way out, I noticed the side of the pavement in front of the Arrival Hall was marked by double zigzag lines. I knew what that meant, since it was tested in the license exams:

No stopping at all times!

$2 ERP

In the morning, I took a man from Bukit Merah to Shenton Way. The fare was $6 and change. He gave me $10, and I returned $3 and change. After some time, the man returned and found me at the taxi stand waiting behind several other taxis. At first, I thought he had left something in my car. But he approached me and said, "You forgot to collect the ERP charges," and handed me a $2 note.

Oops, I did it again.

I had done this many times, but this was the only time a customer returned the money to me, not to mention he had already gone a distance away.

I didn't need to know anything else about him to know that he was a good man.

Mar 2009
31
Tuesday

An Old Working Lady

Late at night, I picked up an old lady in Chinatown to go to West Coast. I asked her what she was doing at this hour and she said she was working. I was surprised as she looked well over seventy. I asked why she had to work late into the night and she told me her story.

She came to Singapore with her family in 1942 from Sichuan, China, when she was nine. Her husband had passed away some years ago. For some reason she didn't live with her children. Instead, she bought a small HDB flat for herself in West Coast after her husband died. Because of her age, the flat had to be paid up in ten years. She had to pay over $1,000 a month for the mortgage. She didn't want support from her children because "they have their own flat to pay for". She earned $50 a day by working in a restaurant as a cook.

She spoke like a woman who was old but not weak, alone but not forlorn, poor but not without dignity.

I have a soft spot for people like her. I have more respect for them than those who sit high on the social pyramid and have everything: wealth, power, fame, or whatever they mean by the term "success", revolve around them. Behind the glorious skyscrapers and ravishing neon lights, thousands and thousands of people in this city live like this old woman. They have nothing outside but they are strong inside. They live at the bottom of society, but they are the very foundation of it. Without their strength and endurance, this nation, no matter if it is a first or second world country, and no matter how many gold or silver medals it wins in the Olympics, and no matter how many hundreds of billions of dollars it has in its reserves, will inevitably collapse.

At the end of the trip, I wanted to discount her fare but she insisted in paying the full amount.

Apr 2009
2
Thursday

Out Of Innocence

Shortly after midnight, a young Chinese lady flagged down my taxi on Balestier Road. After I stopped, she lowered her head and peered through the window for a second before opening the door. She came in, sat in the front seat, and told me in Mandarin to take her to "You Chi".

"You mean Yew Tee, the oil pond?" I asked.

"No," she said. "You Chi, the KTV."

I didn't know of a KTV with that name. I asked her if she knew where it was and she took out a phone and got somebody on the line. "Let my landlord speak to you," she said as she passed the phone to me.

A man with a hoarse voice at the other end of the line said in English, "Take the girl to Orchard KTV in Orchard Towers as quickly as you can, and tell her I am waiting there." The tone was bossy and loaded with impatience. I could also hear noisy music in the background.

"Okay," I replied.

I gave the phone back to the girl and headed towards Orchard Towers.

The girl appeared to be in her early twenties. She was dressed in jeans and a T-shirt, and looked endearing in an innocent kind of way. The fact that she pronounced "Orchard" as "You Chi" indicated to me that she was new to the town and couldn't speak English, which also explained why she checked the driver before she got into the taxi. She had to make sure I spoke Mandarin.

Along the way the girl confirmed that she just arrived three days ago from Fujian, China. She came to Singapore because she believed what she was told by some middle agents that she could make money here. "They told me I can work here in Singapore earning an equivalent of at least eight thousand Renminbi a month," she said.

But it had first cost her and her family RMB60,000 to come. And after she came, she was very disappointed to know there was no job paying RMB8,000 waiting for her. No job at all, in fact.

I asked, "Why don't you just go back?"

"I am stuck," she said moodily. "My family, my parents, are in deep debt now. I have to stay here to find a job to repay the money they borrowed for me."

I had heard similar stories before. I sighed to myself.

But then, her eyes lit up. "Luckily, my landlord is a kind man and he's helping me find a job." She smiled at me. "He has arranged an interview for me tonight. That's where I am going to now. If they like me, I will be working in a KTV as a waitress, as soon as today."

"I am sure they will like you," I murmured. I started to have a bad feeling about this.

"It is not something I had in mind, but it will buy me some time," she added, her smile still visible.

After a short silence I asked, "How did you know your landlord? I mean, how did you find him?"

"Oh, he was introduced to me by the middle agent,"

she replied.

That made sense. I nodded to myself.

I was again quiet for a while, not sure what to say to her. Towards the end of the trip, I decided to say something which I was certain if I kept to myself, I would feel bad for the rest of the night.

I told her that during my month of taxi driving, I had driven several young and good-looking girls like her from China. Some of them, also like her, had paid hefty prices, some fifty or sixty thousand Renminbi, to the middle agents to come to Singapore with the belief they could work here and make more money than they could in China, only to find out when they got here that there was no such job in Singapore, especially a Singapore in its worst economic crisis. The girls I met all ended up selling themselves to Chinese-speaking men, because they, like her, could not speak any English. "You shouldn't trust your landlord," I cautioned, "as you shouldn't have trusted your agent, because I think they are in this together. Melons of the same vine."

"I don't want to sound overly negative," I added in the end. "But just think about it. What's the odds of getting a normal job in Singapore without being able to speak a single word of English?"

She had kept her lips compressed into a thin line while she listened. After I finished, she took a deep breath and said, "Thanks for telling me all this. I appreciate it. I know how to protect myself."

"You'll need to. It is a jungle out there," I said.

Orchard Towers was beside us now. A huge neon signboard on the side of the building lit the street below, which was crowded with partygoers. As the girl handed me the taxi fare, I noticed her hand trembled slightly. I knew she was still excited or nervous about the coming "interview". I wished her luck as she stepped out of the car.

Perhaps she had also stepped out of her innocence, I hoped.

Apr 2009
4
Saturday

Boy Friends

(1)

After a month of driving I have greatly improved my knowledge of routes and places around the city. During the past few days all my trips went smoothly, and I had not encountered a single customer who was dissatisfied with my service.

This evening, I drove a white man from Telok Ayer to Cathay Theater. At one point he asked how long I had been driving a taxi. I invited him to venture a guess.

"At least 15 years, I would say." His tone was sincere.

"What makes you think so?" I asked dryly, trying to hide my smile.

"Oh, I can feel it," he answered. "You have got the look."

"The look of an old taxi driver, eh?"

"Um… the look of someone who knows his way well, I guess."

"Thanks for the compliment." I finally grinned. "But you are wrong this time."

(2)

After midnight, took two young men from East Coast to Bukit Merah. They had apparently just finished their late supper, as they carried a thick smell of food into the car. They both looked to be in their early twenties, one slightly older than the other.

The older boy was playing a Playstation Portable (PSP) using both hands while he talked absently with the younger one, mostly about his games. He seemed to know a great deal about electronic games and, while playing with the gadget in his hands, went through what he liked and disliked about a variety of games. Game design, graphics, level of difficulty, all flowed out of him so effortlessly like a stream running downhill. I couldn't help being amazed at how much time some kids spend on these things nowadays.

The younger boy, on the other hand, appeared to be less tech-savvy. Most of the time, he just listened. When he did speak, he spoke softly and carefully. Somewhere between the monologues of the older boy he asked, "How come you know so much about these things?"

"Because I am interested in them," the older boy said, his eyes still glued to the bright screen.

"Are you interested in *me*?" the younger boy asked, gingerly.

"No," the other answered immediately, "I am not interested in you."

After a short moment of silence, the older boy resumed his natural rate of speech. "You should try this game. It is really good. It takes the graphics to a whole new level…"

The younger boy continued to be an attentive listener and occasionally asked short questions in his soft voice.

As if nothing had happened.

At their destination, they said goodnight to each other and parted company.

For a moment, I felt a hint of sadness for the younger boy. I didn't know why.

Hot Gentlemen, Cold Ladies

(1)

In the late evening at around 9:30pm, three men, two Caucasians and one Singaporean Chinese, boarded my taxi on Shenton Way outside a nightclub. They had come from a drinking party and were heading for another one at a hotel in Chinatown. Well dressed in business attire, they were all in their early thirties and carried an aura of superiority and self-satisfaction, typical of young and smart professionals on the way up their career ladders. Life had treated them well.

The Singaporean guy, probably the youngest and surely the shortest among them, was in the middle of his speech when they got into the car, "…200 ringgit a bottle, you know, that's cheap. The girls, seventy ringgits an hour. That's what, thirty sing. Right? You can have them for the whole night if you like, also very cheap…"

"Sounds like KL is a great place to party," said the white man sitting beside me with a half-empty Heineken bottle in his hand, nodding in agreement.

The animated Singaporean was unfinished. "But it is the Singapore girls that's the best. There's just no

67

comparison…"

"Yeah, but they are not cheap," the white man at the back interrupted. "Singapore girls are fantastic but expensive."

After some debate on Singapore girls, their interest became focused on a lady who was among the people they mingled with earlier in the pub. They all agreed that the woman was the hottest babe in the club that night. Their multi-angled analyses of the woman were sophisticated and rigorous enough to earn my respect for their ability to make acute and penetrating observations, a valuable skill in any profession. Before the hormonal fire inside them could blaze any further, however, the Singaporean man dumped cold water on it by saying that the lady was a friend of a friend, and was already married. That brought to a conclusion both their short-lived fantasies and the trip itself.

The meter displayed a fare of $5 something and they gave me $6 while making their way out. I said, "Wait a minute, there is an extra $3 surcharge."

The Singaporean looked at me with the straightest face and widest eyes he could possibly make, and said, "What surcharge? Why it's not shown on your meter?"

"Sorry about that," I cursed silently before answering. "The meter is an old type but I can give you a receipt with the surcharge on it."

"Forget it," the men responded in unison. "We are not going to pay anything that's not on the meter." With that, they stepped out of the car.

"Hey guys," I called after them, employing the best knowledge of diplomacy I had. "You can't do this to me. Try to be fair, will you?"

The Heineken guy came back in and said to me, "I

live here so I know what you said is correct. But if I were a tourist, I would just tell you to fuck off. Know what I mean?"

I stared at him, in a way a cobra stares at a mongoose. Privately, however, I was unsure what to do: to escalate the issue, or to let it go. At this moment, the Singaporean guy who was now standing on the steps at the hotel's entrance yelled, "Come on. Hurry up. Just ignore him."

Before I blinked my eyes, the young white professional promptly cooled down the air between us. "Look, you are a nice man. I am not actually trying to offend you. I meant if I were... Never mind, here is your three dollars. But you should go back to your company and tell them to fix the meter. That's a very good piece of advice for you, boss."

"Well, thanks." I looked down and took the money. "But I can't even remember how many times I..."

My voice trailed off. The man went out and shut the door before I could finish my sentence.

"...have told them."

(2)

On my way home around 1am, I passed by the Cantonment Police Headquarters and saw three ladies standing by the roadside under the shadow of trees, waiting for a taxi. I stopped and picked them up. Two of them were Chinese and one was Indian, or looked to be. One of the Chinese women sat in the front seat and asked me in a northern Chinese accent to take them to Lorong xx in Geylang .

She was probably in her late twenties, though it was difficult to guess her age with certainty in the hazy yellowish glow of the street lights. She leaned her head against the window with eyes closed and arms folded from the moment she settled in, and looked tired and worn out.

As I turned around to head to Geylang, she opened her eyes and said faintly, "Uncle, can you turn off the aircon, please?"

"Sure, I can turn it down a little."

"No, please just turn it off. I am freezing to death."

"Okay, okay." I turned the air-conditioning off right away.

I was perplexed as I drove along. Being a role model in cost saving vehicle maintenance, my car wasn't really effectively air-conditioned. The air outside was stagnant and heavy with moisture, and the temperature dropped only a few precious degrees since the sun reluctantly went down. This was one of those warm, humid, and breezeless tropical nights we have here for a good part of the year. Just another day in paradise, and yet the ladies were freezing to death.

I peeked at her. Then I thought I knew why.

"So, what happened?" I asked, after driving in silence for a while.

She sat up, looking a lot better than a few moments ago. "You are from China, too?" She answered my question with a question, as she smoothed her hair with both hands.

"Yes, but I have been here before it snowed last time." I bantered and then asked again, "What happened to you today?"

"Ah," she sighed. "We got busted. We were put in a room as cold as an ice cave in the building back there since seven o'clock."

"What have you done? Why did they arrest you?"

"They swept our whole street and arrested at least seventy girls tonight. I was on my way to the coffee shop to eat my dinner when someone in plain clothing grabbed my hair from behind and demanded to see my papers. He took my papers and put me in a van and took us all here."

This surely fit with my own sighting of caravans of police cars and detention vans around the Geylang area in recent days. There appeared to be some major crackdowns going on.

"Are you staying in Singapore illegally?" I asked.

"I have a white card."

I didn't know what that was but I let it go.

"You can't legally work here as, you know, what you do, can you?"

"If I don't stand on the street, how can I survive? I need to pay for the rent and food. Don't I?"

I had no answer to that and remained silent.

After a while, she broke the silence. "Are you a PR now?"

"Citizen," I replied. "You have to be a citizen to be able to drive this thing."

"Taxi driver is not a bad job," she said under her breath, and stared off into the distance, far beyond anything in sight.

"Well," I tried to lighten up the atmosphere a little, "you sound like I have an alternative. I wish I had. But I can't find anything else to do. So as a man, this is my only option."

She turned to me and smiled. "You mean if you were a woman, you could have one more option to choose from?"

"Ha! You got me there," I said lightheartedly. "But the answer is still no. I would still be too old for that."

She burst into laughter…

Aircon Breakdown

My ageing air-conditioner finally quit on me around 6pm, right in the middle of a busy holiday (Good Friday) evening. It had struggled for some time, and lately had given me warning signs. In the last few days, I noticed the air coming out of the dashboard vents was occasionally a little warmer than usual. So I anticipated every breeze it sent out could well be its last.

It was impossible to accept passengers without air-conditioning in this hot and humid weather. I called the Driver Assistance Hotline. The lady who answered my call said I needed to deposit the car in the company's workshop to get my down time rebate, even though nobody would do anything with it until tomorrow. I said fine and drove all the way to Woodlands. The onset of my down time was recorded at 8:30pm.

I took the MRT home and had a relaxed evening with my family.

Yesterday's Customer Once More

(1)

I passed through Chin Swee Road around 10pm and was stopped by two young men. One of them came close and asked me in an unnatural girly voice where the nearest MRT station was. I lowered the window, pointed in the direction of Outram Park MRT station and said, "Over there. It's very close."

"Would you be so kind as to send us there?" He added more sugar to his voice this time.

"What do you mean by send you there? Free of charge?" I shot a glance at him out of the corner of my eye as I answered. He was no older than twenty-five, wearing a short black T-shirt and a pair of tight pants in the same color. Thin and light, he looked like he could be carried to Sumatra by a gust of wind.

"Yes," he said. "Would you?"

"Sorry, young man. Exercise is good for you." I closed the window and started to move. "And makes you a man."

(2)

According to my yet-to-be-verified theory, when people ride with a taxi driver, many of them tend to drop the masks they normally wear on other social occasions. They don't bother to pretend to be somebody they are not. They don't pretend, for example, to be more gracious or more cultivated than they really are, as they would when they are working or socializing. There are several reasons for this. One of them is that a ride with a particular taxi driver is a chance encounter that is unlikely to be repeated, excluding the commuters who use taxis regularly. The chance of randomly picking up the same customer on the street for a second time should be much rarer than hitting a triple seven on a slot machine.

But you never know.

Tonight after midnight, a middle-aged man boarded my taxi on Anson Road. He sat in the front seat and told me to go to Sengkang. "Which way you like me to take?" I asked, as I started moving.

"Hey, I know you," he exclaimed. "You, you are the professor, right?"

I took a look at him and recognized him too. I drove him before, in my beginning days of taxi driving, though I couldn't immediately recall where I picked him up. "I am glad to see you again," I said with a genuine smile.

"You still remember where I live, don't you?" He asked.

"Um, not really. But I guess I can take the ECP and KPE?"

"Anyway you like," he said joyously.

On the way, he talked with me as though I was an old friend of his. He said he remembered the last time he took my taxi, I had no idea how to get him home. He was soaked with beer that night and had a terrible headache. But he fought to stay awake in order to direct me to the right route. I said it was unbelievable how he still remembered things so well even though he was drunk as a skunk at the time.

"Oh yeah," he said, "I still remember a lot of things you told me last time, like how you become a cabdriver from a professor and so on."

When we were near the KPE entrance, he said, "Don't turn in. Just keep going straight."

"Going straight is to go to the airport," I said.

"Doesn't matter. Later you turn to PIE and TPE. Let's take a long ride."

"That will be at least twice as long, you know," I said. "Why would you want to do that?"

"I want to have more time to talk to you," he said.

"Nah, it's too late now," I turned into the KPE just in time, despite his instructions. "We will meet again. I am sure of that."

Where There Is Luck, There Is A Way

In the afternoon, on the busy street of Jalan Bukit Merah, a teenage girl in a student uniform stopped me. She quickly got into the car and said in an anxious, trembling voice, "Uncle, can you take me to ACJC as fast as possible, please?"

"Er, what's ACJC?" I asked casually, trying to calm her down. "Do you know where it is?"

"It's Anglo Chinese Junior College, somewhere near Buona Vista." She was even more nervous now and her voice became half-crying. "Please hurry up, uncle. I am very late." My demonstration of a lack of sense of urgency had done just the opposite of what I intended to do.

I started to move.

"Late for class?" I asked.

"No, late for competition. Is it possible to get there in five minutes?"

"You're joking. You can't get there in five minutes by a helicopter."

"Oh…" she groaned, and buried her face in her hands.

I looked at my watch. 4:45pm. I asked the girl what time her competition was and she answered in a sobbing voice that it was at five o'clock but she had to be there at least five minutes in advance to register.

I contemplated. The traffic was the heaviest at this time of the day, and there was a long way to go before I would see the signboard with "Buona Vista" written on it. The situation appeared hopeless. There was no way I could make it in time. But I had to give it a try.

What was it that people always said when they got lucky?

Where there is a will, there is a way.

Yes, we got lucky. We happened to be near the entrance of an expressway, the AYE, which at the time happened to be not too crowded in the direction we were heading. And after the expressway, on Buona Vista Road, we happened to have green lights waiting for us at all the (four or five) junctions we passed through. We reached ACJC eight minutes before five.

"You still have plenty of time," I said merrily to the girl, as I came to a stop in front of the school.

She didn't seem to have heard me, as she said nothing back, not even a thank you. She just gave me the money, got out and ran past the gate. She had probably forgotten about me even before she unbuckled her seatbelt.

Still, I felt very good as I drove away.

Home Away From Home

"Can you take me to Geylang, please?" A white man in his mid-fifties said to me after he boarded my taxi in Chinatown. The time was 9:50pm.

"Where in Geylang? It is a big place," I said.

"Where the tigers are."

"Tigers?"

"Thai, girrrls," the man repeated one more time, trying to make it right with his heavily accented English.

"I am sorry but I have no idea where they are, sir." I was telling the truth.

"You have no idea, huh?" He said with a sly grin. He was apparently in a very good mood. "In that case, just take me to Lorong xx. I think it's Lorong xx. Yeah, that's where I went last time, if I remember correctly. A taxi driver brought me there."

"Okay, anything you say." I started driving towards Geylang.

On the way, I told him I was a new driver and didn't know many places in the city. I am particularly poorly educated on the *fun* side of the city.

"I am sure you will learn very fast." He laughed.

"Are you here visiting or working?" I asked.

"Working. They made me work here for three months this year. Next year, maybe more. But I don't mind."

"So you like Singapore. Where are you from?"

"I am from Germany. Yes, I *love* Singapore. It's a great place." He sounded like he was telling the truth as well.

"Yes, it is, especially for people like you," I said.

He didn't seem to notice my sarcasm, or care if he did, and went on, "In Singapore, you can find Chinese girls, Thai girls, Indonesian girls, Vietnamese girls, and girls from many other countries. But I like Thai girls best. They are very gentle and lovely."

I wasn't listening anymore. My mind flashed back to the last time I visited Thailand. It must have been ten years ago. We took a trip to Pattaya, a beautiful place with nice and pleasant people, all "very gentle and lovely". Our trip coincided with the time the American aircraft carrier *Kitty Hawk* docked there. We saw big banners hanging on the buildings along the street saying: "WELCOME, AMERICAN SOLDIERS!" It was a long-standing tradition in Pattaya that dated from the time of the Vietnam War. Pattaya's economy boomed during those days. I heard that many nightspots doubled their fees.

There is no doubt that Singapore's economy depends on foreigners too. Americans, Germans, British, Australians, and many others. We welcome them with open arms. We welcome them here to invest, to manage, to consult, to teach, to do whatever they are thought to be good at. We welcome them by making them feel at home.

As a matter of fact, many expatriates, like this gentleman from Germany, feel much better here than they do at home.

Mutual Understanding

(1)

In the afternoon peak hours, a European man in his mid-thirties boarded my taxi at the International Business Park in Jurong East and told me to go to the Riverview Hotel. He looked exhausted from work.

"Tuesday night must be boring in Singapore, huh?" He said with a lazy, European-accented voice, after making himself comfortable in the back seat.

"Depends," I replied absently, while keeping my eyes on the traffic in front of me. "In some parts of town, every night is Friday night."

I had no idea why I said that. Maybe I was just trying to be nice to a hard-working foreigner, or maybe I was just making a conversation. At any rate, I immediately wished I hadn't said it, because I am not exactly very knowledgeable in that topic.

The man promptly bounced from the back seat and arched his body forward so that he could hear my next answer clearly. "Tell me, boss, where can I get sexual massage?" He asked the question as if he was asking about the best chicken rice stall in town.

I knew this was coming. I rolled my eyes at him and

answered reluctantly, "My guess would be Geylang."

"What nationalities are the girls there?" His interest grew more intense.

"All kinds. Chinese, Thai, Indonesian. You name it." I put in use what I learned from a German customer just a few days ago.

"Can you find me a place that has Japanese girls?"

"Well, that's a very good question." I paused. The German guy never mentioned anything about Japanese girls. After a moment of appearing to be thinking really hard, I said, "Sorry, I can't think of any place like that."

Unimpressed, he sank back into his seat and didn't say much after that.

The fare at the end was $15.20. He gave me two $10 notes and asked, "I don't suppose you could give me a twenty cent discount?"

"I would, if you give me a $5 tip," I replied.

"No, no, no." He shook his head like he had just come out of a swimming pool. "Not this time. Not in the middle of the economic crisis."

"Fine. So we understand each other." I grinned at him, while giving him a $5 note.

He put a twenty cent coin in my hand as he took his change. Then he said goodnight and stepped out.

(2)

Late at night, I picked up three young ladies from Tanjong Katong. One of the ladies keyed something into a mobile phone and showed it to me. It took me a while to decipher the fine letters on the old smudged LCD screen.

"Joo Chiat. Is this where you want to go?" I asked. They chuckled but no words came out of their mouths. I assumed it was.

All three appeared to be in their mid-to-late twenties and were dressed in a similar manner: low-cut tank tops and tight and short jean shorts or skirt. Along with the overdone makeup, their profession was written on their faces in capital letters.

On the way, they spoke with each other in a language that sounded completely alien to me. I tried to speak English with them and they just chuckled, without a spoken response.

"Where are you come from?" I asked. They giggled to each other and said something to me in their own language. I didn't know any of their words, and it was apparent that they didn't know mine either.

"Where is your *home*?" I tried again, but was only met with more chuckles.

"*Home*. Your don't know home?"

No response.

"Where are your mama and papa?"

Bingo, they understood this time.

"Vietnam," they said in unison, followed by yet another burst of giggles.

That was all I was interested in knowing. I drove along quietly after that. But I had also learned something else. In some parts of town, the official language used in daily business was not English, Chinese, or any other written and spoken language we know of.

It was *body* language.

The CBD Dilemma

Minutes after 5pm, a middle-aged woman clutching several shopping bags hurriedly flagged down my taxi as soon as she saw me at the Cross Street and South Bridge Road junction. She looked very tired and upset.

"How ridiculous!" she blustered immediately after she got into the car, even before she could catch her breath. "The *whole* Chinatown has no taxis! I waited at the taxi stand over the Indian temple there for more than half an hour and no taxis come! I was so fed up that I was going to walk to the MRT station. Why you people don't want to stop and take passengers? What kind of nonsense is this?"

I had to admit that what she complained about was indeed a problem that has plagued the taxi business here for a long time, a problem nobody seems to have a solution for.

I waited till her anger subsided, then I explained. The reason, I said to her, why some taxi drivers are unwilling to take passengers during the short period prior to 5pm is because both the CBD and peak hour surcharges take effect at this hour. "If we take someone before five, even a second before, we will lose the $3 CBD surcharge."

"If that's what this is all about, why don't they just say so?" She still had a frustrated tone, "I would just *give* them $3 if they had asked, instead of wasting me so much time."

"That would be against the law," I said. "We can't charge you the surcharge when it is not in operation. We could lose our license if we do that."

"You know what?" The lady slapped her thigh loudly, becoming angry again. "I am going to tell everybody not to take taxis from now on."

I forced a smile and said, "That would be terrible for all of us."

Secret Rendezvous

It was almost 10pm. I had been sitting idle at a taxi stand on a small street off Orchard Road for at least twenty minutes. I was beginning to feel the protest of my stomach. The last time I ate anything was eight hours ago. Maybe I should go to eat something now, I thought to myself. But I decided to wait a little longer. This place should have plenty of customers, for the building beside me, as I had known by now, housed some of the best escort service providers in the city.

Only this afternoon, I recalled, I had passed by here to use the washroom in the building. On my way out, I was greeted by a middle-aged woman. Of medium height, she had a fair complexion and looked very well preserved for her age. She asked me in a low voice, "Do you want a girl?"

"I am the one who drives your girls around." I gave her a wide grin as I answered.

She pulled her chin back, stared at me, and frowned in confusion.

"I am a taxi driver," I added.

"Oh, I thought you are someone working in this place." She lost interest in me and walked away.

My reflections were interrupted by the squeaking sound of a door opening. Finally, a customer.

It was a girl in her mid-twenties. She was dressed in a short-sleeved, light colored blouse and a knee-length, floral skirt, and looked charming and delightful. She came in and sat in the back seat and told me to go to Bukit Batok Avenue 6.

"How would you like me to go?" I asked.

"I don't have a lot of ideas myself," she replied. Her accent indicated she was a local. Maybe she worked in one of the offices in the building.

"How do you normally go?" I asked again. The rule of thumb in my line of work is to always take the route the customer prefers, if he or she has one.

"I seldom go from here," she said flatly, which meant my initial postulation was wrong.

I asked her if it was okay to take the AYE by River Valley and then the PIE by Clementi Avenue 6, and she said fine.

On the way, she was busy typing on her cell phone. Every few minutes, her phone chirped, and was followed by her continuous, well-practiced tapping of the keypad. After a dozen or so exchanges between her and whomever she was communicating with, we arrived at Bukit Batok.

"This is East Avenue 6," I said to her. "Where is your place?"

"Just keep moving," she said. The sound of her fingers dancing rapidly on the keypad continued. After a minute or two, a new message arrived and immediately, she said, "It's Block xxx, West Avenue 6." I said okay.

When we were on West Avenue 6, I asked her again where Block xxx was and she said, "I don't know. You just have to look for it."

"You don't live here?"

"No, I don't." Her tone was icy cold. She didn't like the question.

I slowed down and looked hard for numbers on the buildings along the street but I couldn't see any. Wherever they were placed was just not easily visible at night. To make things worse, all the HDB blocks in this area had the same color, same style, and same drab façade.

By this time the girl had stopped her messaging. She sat quietly, staring out of the window, as if she were enjoying a scenic ride along a coastline.

I was still busy turning my head up and down, left and right, looking desperately for the right block when the girl abruptly said, "Stop here."

We were now at the roadside next to an HDB housing block. I looked and saw no numbers on it. "Are you sure this is it?" I asked.

"Yes, I am sure." She uttered the words quickly, paid the fare, got out, and walked briskly into the building.

I was totally knocked out. How on earth did she know? I looked around again. Then I saw it.

A red motorcycle parked under the shadow of a tree, standing halfway between the street and the building.

I had to smile. "Clever guy," I said to myself as I drove away.

Apr 2009

26
Sunday

Three Filipino Maids

In the evening, three ladies boarded my taxi at Lucky Plaza on Orchard Road. Two of them looked to be in their forties and another in her mid-thirties. They told me to take them to Stevens Road.

They apparently had an enjoyable evening, cheerfully talking and laughing during the trip. They spoke English fluently and accurately, with a hint of an American accent. They told me they were from the Philippines and worked here as maids for the same family. I was happy to chat with them and was especially impressed by their remarkable sense of humor that I don't see very often from my customers.

On a small inner street off Stevens Road, we stopped outside a spacious walled residence. Through a wrought iron gate, I had a glimpse of a big mansion surrounded by trees, flowers, and colorful children's play equipment. In front of the main entrance sat two expensive cars, sparkling under the porch light.

"Daddy is home," said one of the ladies, and the other two laughed.

"Who is going to pay me?" I asked amidst their laughter.

"I am," said the one sitting beside me.

Because of the short distance, the fare was only $4.40. As the lady in the front was unzipping her handbag, one from behind stuck some money into my hand. It was a $5 and a $2 note.

I held the $2 up and said, "No need for this one. You can keep that, and…"

Three palms pressed on my hand at the same time. "It's our tip. Please take it," they said together.

"Okay, I will take sixty cents, which is very good already," I said.

"No, please take it all," one of them said before leaving the car. "You've been very nice to us. This is our way to say thank you."

I was truly moved. I get tipped from my customers very rarely, not because my service is poor, but because tipping is just not a way of life here. These ladies only make a few hundred dollars a month but they were among the most generous customers I have ever had.

I let out a long sigh before I drove away.

The Virgin Ride

Late at night, around 1am, I was cruising on Boon Lay Way, heading towards the city. Near Jurong East Central, I saw three men standing in the darkness on the sidewalk. I slowed down as I approached. When I eased by them, they appeared to be uncertain whether they needed a ride. I was just about to pick up speed when one of them jumped on the road behind me and raised his arm. I saw him in the mirror and braked to a stop.

The man waved goodbye to his companions and walked towards me, while the other two each picked up a bicycle from the ground and started to walk away. He came and sat in the front seat and told me to go to Tiong Bahru.

He was in his mid-thirties, wearing a polo T-shirt and a pair of cheap, creased trousers. His hair looked as if it had not tasted shampoo for weeks. Despite the displeasing odor he brought into the car, I was glad to have a customer at last.

Along the way, he told me he was from Myanmar and had been here for one year and seven months. His English was bad but not bad enough to prevent us from having an enjoyable conversation. Today, he said, he came to see his sister's son, one of the men with bicycles I saw just now. By the time they realized it was time for him to go back to his dormitory, it was already too late to take the MRT. "I have never taken a taxi before in my whole life," he said. "This is the first time."

I asked him what he did for a living in Singapore and he said he worked on ships on Jurong Island, earning $500 a month. After meals and phone cards, he had no money left. He worked twelve hours a day and for every four days of work, he got one day off. I told him that in this regard, he was luckier than me. I also worked twelve hours a day, sometimes even longer, but I have no days off. I work seven days a week.

When we reached his dorm, the meter fare was about $19 with the midnight surcharge. From his pocket, he took out what looked to be a currency note folded into a small square, in the size of a beer bottle cap. He slowly unfolded it, as if it were made of some delicate, easy-to-break fabric. It was a $50 note.

"A gift from my nephew," he smiled at me. "He's been here more than four years and he makes $1,200 a month. A rich man." He handed the note to me while holding his smile in place effortlessly.

I smoothed the money between my fingers as I thought about what to do. I quickly made up my mind.

"I know you are a poor man," I said to him, looking into his eyes. "And I am a poor man too. So today we are going to help each other out. Okay?"

He nodded with a timid, uneasy expression on his face.

"I will just take $10 from you. Is it okay with you?"

He opened his mouth but lost his voice. He stuttered something and then said thank you twice in English and twice in Chinese.

"Thank you," I said, "for taking your first taxi ride with me."

The Good, The Bad And The Ugly

(1)

"弱水三千，只取一瓢"

While the river is three thousand miles long, one ladle is all I want

This Chinese proverb was the first thing that flashed in my mind when I found myself the only taxi coming to the rescue of a long line of people, many of whom looked tired and impatient, waiting at the Raffles City taxi stand around 10pm. This is another peculiar thing about the taxi business. Despite the presence of a crowd of customers that seem to be all yours for the taking, you can only do one job at a time. A hundred customers are only as good as one in a taxi driver's equation.

At the head of the queue, I picked up two Singaporean ladies. One was in her mid-twenties. Dressed in a lace blouse and a skirt, with long smooth hair, she looked beautiful. The other one was rounder and clearly older, probably in her early thirties, with shoulder length hair and a dark blue office outfit. After they came in, the younger one said to me, "Uncle, two places. Can?"

"Sure," I answered, as I looked at them in the mirror.

"Toa Payoh first. You can go by CTE," she said. "Then I will let you know how to get to my place. After that, you go to Serangoon Gardens. Okay? Thank you uncle." Her voice was sweet and charming, and reminded me of those young – what's the word? – *coquettish* girls you see every time you tune into these Chinese channels on Starhub TV.

They were talking happily as the journey started. But their voices were soon reduced to whispers, which were further replaced by silent kisses. Though they kept themselves out of the viewing field of the rear-view mirror, the back seat of a taxi was hardly the world's best place for privacy. As I checked my blind spot, I inevitably caught glimpses of them, sinking deeply into each other's arms and tenderness.

"弱水三千". That phrase came up again. This was the sixth or seventh time I had seen affections between women in my car since I started driving. "Where does the river flow nowadays?" I wondered.

The pretty girl finally pulled herself out of her friend's grasp by the time we reached Toa Payoh, and started to direct me to her place on Lorong 4 with her ever so sweet and soft voice. With such a voice, I thought, she could definitely cure diseases in the hospitals.

After the pretty girl kissed her friend goodbye and left the car, the climate changed immediately from summer to winter. Speaking to me for the first time, the office lady told me, dryly and coldly, to go to Serangoon Gardens, while striving as hard as she could to make a long face out of a round one. She suddenly acted as if I had somehow offended her.

That was enough to make me nervous. I gathered all my energy to focus on driving, fearing that the slightest mistake on my part might give her the opportunity to lash out at me.

As I gingerly maneuvered into Serangoon Garden Way via Lorong Chuan, the lady began to direct me to her place with abrupt and blunt instructions. After countless turns and endless narrow driveways, I was finally relieved to hear her say "stop here". She paid the fare without any eye contact and stepped out without saying thank you.

On my way back to the city, I searched my soul for any trace of anything I might have done to make the second lady mad and I really couldn't find any. My final conclusion was that before they boarded my taxi, they had shared an ice cream at Haagen Dazs. The pretty girl ate all the vanilla and this lady had all the nuts.

(2)

A few hours later at around 2am, I came by one of the city's most popular nightspots, a small street in Chinatown, on my last round of cruising before heading home. The strip is not long but is crowded with bars and nightclubs, open late into the wee hours well after most other places have turned off their lights.

As I eased through the narrow one-way street, compressed into an even thinner pathway by cars parked on each side, I heard someone shouting frantically. Suddenly, a young Asian man leaped onto the road right in front of my car. He was in his early twenties, small and thin, and would have looked very feeble and fragile, *if he were not waving a knife in the air and shouting angrily.*

A small group of men and women immediately followed him. Someone tried to grab the knife but failed. Then a white man about six feet tall emerged from another direction, with blood all over his face. He staggered towards the roadside, where I saw another white man crouched low, leaning against a column and seemingly in great pain. A young Asian girl who had tried to calm down the boy a moment ago was now on her cell phone, probably speaking to an emergency operator.

At this time, some cars honked loudly from behind. I looked back and saw a string of cars stalled behind me. I started to move. I turned to the main road. After a few minutes, I decided to drive back to the scene to take another look. I was curious to find out what was going on.

Nothing was going on now. Five to ten minutes later, everyone had vanished from the street.

There was no boy with a knife in his hand.

There was no white man with blood on his face.

There was no girl with a cell phone to her cheek.

And there was no police car or ambulance to be found.

There were just a few men standing at a pub's entrance, smoking and chatting. The way they looked, they were more likely talking about stocks they would like to buy when the market opened a few hours later, than some ugly, bloody fights that had happened minutes ago.

It was time for me to go home.

For Sentimental Reasons

As usual, after the evening peak hours ended at 8pm, commuters who had shunned taking taxis in the past three hours because of the 35% surcharge started to flock to various taxi stands in the central areas. Today, this temporary surge in demand for taxis seemed to be particularly palpable, perhaps because it was a holiday eve.

I drove by the Outram Park MRT station shortly after eight and saw a very long queue, at least twenty or so people, waiting at the taxi stand. I knew they would have to wait there for quite a while, since that was probably the least favored place for most taxi drivers to pick up passengers at this time of the day.

But I stopped at the head of the queue without a second thought.

A young Asian man boarded my taxi and told me to go to the airport. "Please take the quickest way, uncle," he said. "I am really, really late." Though he was trying his best to look calm and collected, his voice was tense, anxious, weary, and relieved, all at once.

He was dressed neatly, in what could be referred to as "smart casual": a short sleeved shirt and a pair of cotton trousers. He carried a midsized suitcase which he graciously declined to put in the trunk. Overall, he projected an aura of maturity and composure, although I was certain he was no older than thirty.

"What time is your flight?" I asked, as I was driving towards the ECP.

"Nine o'clock. Do you think we can make it? It's ten past eight now." The anxiety in his voice was easily detectable.

"Should be able to, if there is no jam on the highway," I answered, knowing that it didn't help him very much.

He told me he was from the Philippines and on his way back to Manila. He had waited at the taxi stand for more than half an hour. "I saw many taxis passing by and all of them carried no passengers. Why they don't want to stop for us?" he asked, probably more out of annoyance than curiosity.

"It is because that taxi stand is too close to CBD, the Central Business District," I answered. "They drive five more seconds, they will be inside CBD, where they will get extra three dollars as the CBD surcharge from the passengers."

"It's very nice of you, uncle, to stop there," he said.

We soon found out that our wish for a smooth ride on the highway was far-fetched. Soon after we got onto the ECP from Keppel Road, the traffic started to halt. In five minutes, we moved a distance shorter than if we had walked, no, shorter than if we had crawled.

The situation, as grave as it looked, was pushing the young man to the edge.

"How long you think this jam will last, uncle?" he asked, agitatedly.

Just then, I saw the electronic message board. The digital letters spelt: "MASSIVE JAM TILL MARINE

PARADE." He saw that too.

"Marine Parade is too far away," I said to him. "This is not gonna work. We need to change plan."

I told him our only hope would be to take the KPE, which was not far ahead, and get to the airport by the PIE, provided there was no congestion over there. He said he would leave it to me to decide.

As I moved with much difficulty, and some ungraciousness, to the extreme left lane, I found the flow of traffic was better there, because some of the cars on this lane were exiting to the KPE. It didn't take us long to reach the entrance of the KPE tunnel.

Luckily, I made the right decision. The traffic on the KPE and PIE was indeed much lighter. I drove as fast as I could and arrived at the airport twenty minutes before nine.

"Thank you, uncle. I owe you," he said to me as he handed me the fare, after we stopped at the departure hall of Terminal One.

"No, you don't," I replied. "And if you really feel thankful, thank your fellow countryman."

"Okay." He flickered a glance of confusion at me. But he had no time, and no mood, to fancy my riddle. He took his suitcase and rushed into the building.

I was smiling as I drove away. I felt good, though I didn't have a chance to tell him the reason I stopped for him at that taxi stand. It is not because I am a particularly nice guy. I *always* stop at that taxi stand, whenever I pass by. It holds a special place in my heart. It is the location where I served my first customer on my first day as a taxi driver. He was nice to me even after I made a mistake and took the wrong way.

And he happened to be Filipino too.

Life Is A Highway

While I was waiting in the taxi queue at the Budget Terminal of the airport this evening, a yellow Toyota from Citicab joined the queue behind me. The driver, in his late fifties or early sixties, got out and ambled over when he saw me smoking by my taxi. He lit his cigarette and asked, "How is your day?"

I knew what he wanted to hear but I said, "Fine. How is yours?"

"Not bad." He turned his head slightly and exhaled a long trail of smoke with a smile. "I came out at noon and already got $180 in my pocket," he said, volunteering his report card first.

"That's fantastic." I conveyed my performance to him indirectly. "$180 in seven hours? How did you do it?"

"I was lucky. I got seven calls today."

The Citicab and Comfort taxi companies have a de facto monopoly of the on-call booking market in Singapore. This makes a big difference. Seven calls equal $21 extra.

I told him I was a new driver. During my two month driving career, I never received any calls from my company. What he made in seven hours was what I would hope to make in twelve.

He was quick to console me. He said business was generally bad at present. He had been driving for more than five years and had never seen things as bad as now. He usually made $50 or so a day after costs. Sometimes just $10 or $20. "My kids have all grown up and don't need my support," he said. "Sometimes I go back after I made enough for a pack of cigarettes. I don't have to work as hard as the other guys." He pointed his jaw at the cabbies standing and chatting along the taxi queue ahead of us.

"Eight out of ten of them are not healthy," he continued. "Kidney, heart, stomach, bowel. All kinds of problems. I have several friends who quit driving because of that."

He said he knew a lot of old-timers who had quit because of the harsh working conditions and the difficulty of earning a living. "That's why many newcomers like you can have a chance to try out your luck," he said with a friendly grin.

I didn't know what to say and remained silent.

He ditched his cigarette butt and was ready to move. "I am not going to wait here. Waste of time. I am going back now." He shook my hand and walked to his car.

I was driving on the highway back to the city a few minutes later. The man was right that it was a bad idea to wait in a queue that never moved. The traffic on the ECP in this direction was light. Cruising smoothly along the coast with refreshing plants and flowers greeting me from the roadside, I was in a good mood.

True, life is hard, especially after a transition from a lifelong scientist to a rookie taxi driver. But life is like this highway: sometimes smooth, sometimes rough; sometimes you go slow, sometimes you go fast; sometimes it frustrates you, sometimes it pleases you. As long as you know where you are going, and never quit halfway, you will get there sooner or later.

Lord Ye Loved Dragons

This afternoon, a middle-aged woman boarded my taxi on Orchard Road. She told me to go to Tanjong Katong.

After a period of silence, she said abruptly, "I am so sad today."

I looked at her in the mirror and asked, "What happened?"

"My bird died this morning. The poor little thing strangled himself," she said with a grief-stricken expression.

"Sorry to hear that," I said.

She continued on about how much she loved the bird and how shocked she was this morning to see the bird dead, dangling mid-air in the cage with a string around his neck.

After she finished her monologue, she stared in my direction for a moment. "You don't look like an ordinary cabdriver."

"I am a bona fide ordinary cabdriver," I said. "Only I haven't been one for long."

In the next ten minutes, I told her how I went from scientist to cabdriver. She was unimpressed. "Maybe it's because you are too proud. It's a lesson for you."

"Do you know the Chinese story called 'Lord Ye loved

dragons'?"

"No," she said.

Once upon time in China, I started to tell her, there was a rich man named Lord Ye. He let the whole world know that he loved dragons. Everything in his magnificent house was decorated with sculptures or paintings of dragons. The bed he slept on, the bowls he ate from, the table in his study, the pavilion in his garden, everything. Dragons were his passion. Eventually, this news was passed on to a real dragon. "Lord Ye seems to be a really nice guy to be with," the dragon thought to himself. "I bet he will be thrilled to see me coming to stay with him." The dragon decided to fly to Lord Ye's home. But Lord Ye was not at all happy to see him. He was frightened at the sight of the real dragon and shouted, "Get out of here!"

"You are saying you are a real dragon," the woman said sarcastically at the end of my story.

"I am speaking of a metaphor in general terms," I said.

"Well," she said, softening her tone. "Why don't you go somewhere else, where you can use your talent? You are from China, right? Why not go back to China? Seems to be an exciting place to be at present. I want to leave myself. It's too hot for me here. Never got used to it." After a pause, she spoke suddenly in her mourning tone again: "Oh, my poor bird. Made me feel so sad for the whole day."

That was the end of our conversation.

A Drunk Man

It was 2:30am in the morning. I was on my way home when I saw a man wobbling along Cross Street in Chinatown. He stopped me and threw himself into the back seat, murmuring "Ang Mo Kio Avenue 9".

After I arrived at Ang Mo Kio Avenue 9 I asked, "Where is your place?" But there was no answer. I turned and found the man sound asleep. I pitched my voice higher as I repeated the question. It was no use. He was as motionless as a hibernating bear. I pulled over at the curb and got out of my seat.

I opened the door to the back seat, and patted his shoulder. "Wake up, man." There was no response. I patted harder but still could not wake him up. I tried to set him upright but it proved to be a difficult task. The man was about my height but was much wider and heavier. With all the energy I had left in me after a long day of work, I finally put him in a sitting position. The man, his head drooped forward, remained as sound asleep as a newborn baby.

I didn't know what to do now. I looked around. The street was quiet and deserted. I stopped the meter first – it seemed awfully inappropriate to charge him for his sleeping time. Then I lit a cigarette and contemplated my options. After a while, another taxi appeared. I leapt forward to stop it, and told the driver of a Comfort taxi that I got a drunk customer in my car who couldn't be awakened. I asked him what he would suggest me to do. "Call the police" was all he said before he sped off.

"Call the police." That seemed to be the solution to all the problems we taxi drivers have. As I was thinking about it, a phone rang. It was the man's phone. I hastily searched his pockets and found the phone.

"Hi." It was a woman's voice.

"Hello," I said gratefully, "I am the taxi driver with your friend here. He is sleeping and I can't wake him up. Do you know where his home is?"

The woman said she was so sorry about her husband and asked me to take him to a condo on Avenue 9. "After you reach here, come to block xxx, and I will meet you at the entrance of the building," she said.

The condo was nearby. I went directly to the block the lady specified, and waited. Ten minutes passed and there was still no sight of the woman. I took out the phone from the man's pocket and called her again.

"You are here already?" She sounded surprised. I realized I didn't tell her I was in the neighborhood when we last spoke. "I am coming down now," she said.

A minute later, a woman in her late twenties emerged in shorts and T-shirt. She looked like she had not been sleeping, probably waiting for her husband all night long.

She apologized to me and paid the fare, then went to wake the man in the car. She did everything she could, shaking, pulling, slapping, grabbing, shouting. It was all in vain. The man was as lifeless as a trunk of wood, only now in a level position again.

Exhausted at last, the woman said she would go upstairs to get their maid to help. The maid, who looked to be a Filipino, was more skillful than any of us. She bent down and squeezed the nose of the man and that did the trick. The man finally came back to the real world. He still couldn't walk properly, though. Sandwiched between two ladies, he was half-carried to the elevator.

I looked at my watch. It was almost five o'clock. "What a waste," I sighed, and drove away.

May 2009

12

Tuesday

Indecent Proposal

Around midnight on Jalan Besar, I was flagged down by a young woman. She took the back seat and told me in Mandarin to go to Hougang.

She was in her mid-to-late twenties and wore a tight, light-colored spaghetti strap singlet and pair of denim shorts that were so small they could pass for underwear. Although this was a pretty common outdoor getup among teenage girls in Singapore, it was also the standard dress code for bar girls.

I knew this as I had once driven a KTV girl on a round trip, who was ordered by her boss to go home and change into something "appropriate". She went in jeans and tank top and came back dressed exactly the same way this woman sitting behind me was dressed.

Sure enough, the woman told me she worked in a pub near where I picked her up. Today, she said, business was very slow. The pub was almost empty the entire evening. As she didn't get to sit with customers, she was asked to leave "early".

I was not surprised. "What do you expect on a Tuesday night?" I said nonchalantly. "Worse still, Jalan Besar isn't exactly a hotspot for night owls. Maybe you should switch to somewhere with a better location."

She sighed but said nothing in return. I stole a glance at her in the mirror. She looked like she had fallen into a sea of unhappy memories. I regretted the tone I had just used.

After a few moments, she told me that she had come to Singapore a couple weeks ago from Fujian, China. She didn't know anybody here except for a few folks from her hometown, and she couldn't speak any English. She was able to find a job in this pub only because one of her hometown friends had helped her. The job paid peanuts, relying mainly on handouts from customers, and was very inconvenient to get to by public transport from her place. She paid $300 a month for a bed in a room she shared with two other girls. She was stuck with the working and living conditions she was "blessed" with. She said she told me all this because I was the first taxi driver from China she had met.

I knew too many stories like hers. I knew how they came, how they got stuck, and how they were carried away by the murky undercurrents of this place. I heard these stories time and again, so much so that I had become immune to the tormenting feelings prompted by them. "Yes, I know, I know," I muttered to her as much as to myself.

As I stopped outside her residence, an old condo, the meter showed a fare of $12. She slowly opened her purse while asking me if I could give her a discount. "I didn't get any tips today," she said. "I come home empty-handed."

I thought for a moment and said, "Okay. $10 will do."

She took out a $10 note from her bag and said, "This is all I have. I give you this I will go hungry tomorrow morning."

"I don't believe you," I said. "It can't be that bad."

"You can see for yourself." She opened her bag in front of my face and went through the stuff inside. There were keys, some makeup, a small pack of tissue paper, a phone, and a wallet which contained nothing but some plastic cards. No money. She then patted her pockets, which were set so tightly on her hips that it was obvious there was nothing in there.

She leaned forward and placed her elbows on the top of the front seat and said in an undertone, "You are a nice man. I want to be a friend with you."

I turned and gazed at her. She held my look with a slight smile. I looked away and said, "No matter what you say, you still have to pay for the fare."

"I will be your girlfriend," she said softly into my ear. "All you need to do is just…"

"I am an old man and I don't need a girlfriend." I cut her off.

"Wrong. Old men *especially* need girlfriends!" she said with laughter.

"No," I turned to her again and said forcefully, "I said no! Okay? Just give me the money!"

"You don't like me?" She was startled by my anger and hurriedly took out the $10 and handed it to me.

I took the money, gave her $5 back and said, "This should be enough for your breakfast. Now go home."

She took the money and gave me a long look before stepping out.

I felt I was carrying a terrible weight on my heart as I drove away.

A Forgotten Box

A tall and slim white man in his mid-thirties and a Chinese lady a few years his junior were chitchatting on the side of Anson Road when I stopped in front of them shortly after 8pm. The lady got in first while the guy lifted a cardboard box from the ground and placed it in the trunk. He then came in and told me to go to two places, both of which were on Upper Bukit Timah Road.

Dressed in impeccable business attire, they appeared to be colleagues from the same work place, an accounting firm. He was a European and she a Singaporean. Their conversation was about office politics and the woman did most of the talking. It was obvious to me that she tried her best to impress the guy by showing off what she thought was a sharp and witty perception of what was going on in their firm, viewed from her morally high but emotionally detached vantage point, and presented in carefully decontaminated Singlish. The European guy, being a well bred gentleman, offered his moral support by occasionally saying "yes I agree", "yeah that's true" or words to that effect.

After I dropped them off one after the other, I decided to drive back to the city via Bukit Timah Road. Lately I had set a target of making at least five CBD trips per evening for myself. By adhering to this strategy, my daily earnings had seen a noticeable improvement in recent days. As I stopped before the red light at the Bukit Timah Road and Bencoolen Street junction, staring obliviously at a televised commercial on a giant screen, I suddenly realized that the European man had forgotten to take his box with him when he alighted! I had to go back! I cursed loudly as I made a U-turn to head to where I just came from.

I stopped outside the gate of the condo where I dropped the white man off. I got out and approached the security guard. I asked him if he remembered a tall white man who strode in not long ago. "When's that?" the guard, a Malay man in his fifties, asked as he rolled his eyes at me from the newspaper in front of him.

"About half an hour ago," I said.

"I wasn't here half an hour ago. I just got here no more than ten minutes." He went back to his newspaper before he finished the sentence.

"Who is the guard before you?" I felt I was getting butterflies in my stomach.

"It's a lady," he answered without looking at me.

"Where is she?"

"She is away. She will be back later."

I cursed again as I walked back to the car. I opened the trunk and took out the box. It was heavy. I set it down on the cement ground below the window of the guardhouse and examined it closely.

It was sealed in its original, nondescript packaging. There was no label to indicate what was inside. It seemed to fit the description of "suspicious objects" that the lady in the loudspeakers of the MRT trains and stations constantly reminded us of. But the name of the manufacturer printed on the box suggested it was unlikely an explosive or a biological warfare agent. It was probably some kind of electronic equipment, and an expensive one as well. I thought about leaving it to this security guard, but the idea was immediately overruled. This thing looked too valuable to be entrusted to a guy who paid more attention to his newspaper than to an anxious cabdriver looking urgently for one of his residents. Besides, he could not identify the man this box rightfully belonged to. I had no choice but to wait for the lady guard to return.

My patience grew thinner by the minute. Finally, I approached the male guard again. I asked if he could contact the lady guard by phone and he said he could not. I asked where she had gone to and he said she was in the garage supervising some repair works. I asked him to go get her for me and he said he couldn't leave his post. I said I would watch the gate for him while he was gone and he said he really couldn't do that. I said if he didn't get the lady guard here in one minute I would leave immediately and this resident would be so pissed he would be sure as hell to do everything possible to have him fired. He raised his head to stare at me for a moment to ensure I meant what I said. Then he stood up, walked out of the guardhouse and disappeared into the basement parking garage.

A few minutes later, an Indian lady in a guard uniform hastened towards me from the basement driveway. She asked me what the matter was and I told her I needed to find the white man who came in about thirty to forty minutes ago because he had left his stuff in my taxi. "That ang moh guy? He is always forgetful," she laughed. "You wait here and I go to tell him." She headed to the lift lobby.

In another ten or so minutes, the white man finally emerged. He was wearing a pair of boxer shorts and a

T-shirt and had apparently just gotten out of the shower, with his hair still dripping beads of water onto his cheeks. He waltzed over and said to me in an apologetic tone, "Sorry, I totally forgot about it." He smacked his forehead with an open hand, a gesture meant either to curtail his embarrassment or wipe some water off his face, or both.

"Yeah. Well, I forgot about it, too," I said as I glanced at his outfit.

He stood in front of me, and seemed to be struggling to hold something on the tip of his tongue. His eyes flickered away from me.

"Here is your box," I said to him.

He thanked me, and was about to move over to it when I stalled him by saying, "I know this is as much my fault as it is yours. Nevertheless, since I have come a long way to return it to you, it would be nice if you could…"

"Here, take this," he interrupted me and opened his hand. There was a $10 note lying in the center of his sweaty palm, crumpled in a ball. He had it all along. He briefly straightened the damp note before handing it to me.

I took the money, thanked him, and left.

Biting The Bullet

After midnight a Singaporean man boarded my taxi on Duxton Hill, one of the popular nighttime hangouts in town. He sat in the back seat and told me to go to "Kang Bahru."

His words sounded strange so I sought confirmation. "Are you saying Tiong Bahru, Sir?" He said "Kang Bahru" once again, and added a "yes" at the end. So I started driving towards Tiong Bahru without giving a second thought to his weird pronunciation.

He was of medium height, in his late thirties or early forties, and wore a striped, short sleeved shirt, tucked in a dark colored pair of slacks. In the mirror his face looked puffy and pale. His eyes were lifeless but not sleepy. He fixed his stare on the streets outside the window. There was a smell of alcohol in his breath, subtle but unmistakable.

The route to Tiong Bahru via Cantonment Road was short and straightforward. After I passed Eu Tong Sen Street the man said abruptly, "Hey, where are you going?"

I looked at him in the mirror and said, "You said you are going to Tiong Bahru. Right?"

"Kang Bahru is this way." He pointed to the left.

"No. Tiong Bahru is this way." I pointed straight

113

ahead.

"I never said *Tiong* Bahru! I said *Kang* Bahru…
Kang…*Kampong* Bahru!" He stuttered on the name of the
street for a few seconds before he finally got it right. He
had said it wrong all along.

I braked to a stop and said, "Okay, this is not my fault.
Kampong is a two syllable word and you didn't say it that
way in the beginning." But I didn't want to get on this guy's
nerves at this hour of the night. So I quickly added, "Never
mind. It's not a big deal. I will just make a U-turn now." I
started to move to the right lane to make a U-turn.

"Are you calling me a liar?" the man said belligerently,
and stiffened his body away from the back of the seat,
totally ignoring the goodwill I had shown him.

"I haven't called you anything," I said, trying to
calm him down. "I am only saying if you had told me the
street name correctly, we wouldn't have to make this little
detour."

"Don't you dare argue with me!" the man suddenly
pitched his voice high. "*When I talk to you, you face
down!*"

"What?" I couldn't believe my ears.

I stopped the car, and turned to stare into his eyes,
"What did you just say?"

Like a spear piercing through his forehead, my glare
instantly stunned him and sank him back into his seat.

He gawked at me soullessly and murmured, "What?"

"You said 'when I talk to you, you face down'," I said
through my teeth.

"No, I didn't. I never said that," the man mumbled.
All the aggressiveness he showed a moment ago had
drained dry. He now looked like a ten year old caught for
shoplifting.

I suddenly felt sorry for him. I quickly turned round to the steering wheel, and said, "Forget it. You want to go to Kampong Bahru, right? I take you to Kampong Bahru. Let's just get this over with." I started the car again.

As if a dead fire had come alive again, the man swiftly recovered from his momentary defeat after he realized I was not going to do anything to him. He sat up and started raising his voice again. "So what! Huh? Is 'face down' such a bad word? Is 'face down' such a bad thing to say? *Yes I said that!* So what! Did I ever scold you? Did I ever say fuck you? Huh? Stop the car! Answer me!" He was shouting and screaming hysterically.

No matter how crazy and intimidating he made himself look, I remained silent and continued driving. I decided not to be bothered by him anymore. I knew he was just a "银样腊枪头" (silver blade made of wax), as we call it in Chinese, and I could easily scare the shit out of him again if I wanted to. There is an abundance of this type of people around us, who are like those small puppies that bark at you ferociously when you pass by. As soon as you turn to face them and give them a stern look, they sit back and shut their mouths. Of course, they will jump up and bark at you again after you turn your back to them. To people like this, I always want to turn my back and walk away as quickly as I can. If I ever pause my footsteps and turn around to spook off an annoying, empty threat, it will only be to a cute little puppy dog.

My unresponsiveness to his provocation, however, was only perceived by him as an exhibition of weakness. He pressed home his advantage by escalating the level of intimidation. Now on every screamed word, he slapped his hand forcefully on the top of the leather seat in front of him, making a deafening sound like gunfire next to my ear.

I bit the bullet and kept the car moving.

When I made the turn at the junction, he saw the Cantonment Police Headquarters on the corner. He shouted his slapping-accented demands rhythmically. "Go to the police station! I have got time to deal with you. Go! Go! Turn into the carpark! I order you! Go!"

His hand surely hurt like hell by now.

At the entrance of the police carpark, a policeman was standing on duty. I pulled over next to him and lowered the window. He leaned down and asked me, "Want to come in?"

"He is drunk." Finding comfort in the presence of a policeman, I spoke in a mild and well-composed tone. "And making trouble for me. What should I do?"

"Do you want to file a report?" the policeman asked.

"No. I don't have time for that," I said.

"Officer," the man in the back intervened. "I am not drunk. This driver made a mistake and drove me the wrong way. And he's got a bad temper. He accused me of saying 'face down' to him. Officer, is 'face down' really a bad word?"

"Where do you want to go?" the policeman asked him, ignoring his question.

"Kampong Bahru."

"Are you going to the pubs there?" He pointed to the cluster of colorfully lit shophouses about a hundred yards away.

"Yes."

The policeman now turned to me and said. "Why don't you drop him off there and give him some discount?"

I said I wasn't the one who had a problem with it, and moved on.

Ten seconds later, I stopped outside a bar along

Kampong Bahru. The meter fare was more than $8. I told him he could just pay me $5. He took out a $5 note, but yanked it beyond my grasp when I reached for it. He stared at me and said, "Answer me. Is 'face down' such a bad word?"

"Why don't you just keep your money and get out?" I said to him in a flat voice.

He threw the note on the front passenger seat and said, "Man, I tell you. You've got a *bad* attitude! *Bad, bad attitude!*" He did not seem to want to leave just yet, as if he still had unfinished business with me, but left after a brief moment of indecision.

However despicable his behavior was, which may or may not have been influenced by his blood alcohol concentration at the time, he got away with his abuse of me triumphantly, partly because I let him. I didn't file a police report on him. But even if I did, I doubt it would make any difference. It was ultimately my word against his. He was not drunk, he was not crazy, and he was not stupid. He knew that if it came down to my word against his, he would be in a sure-win position. The fact that he hysterically "ordered" me to go to the police station showed how confident he was that he would be favorably taken care of by the system, counting on his higher social status to give his words more credibility than that of a cabdriver in the eyes of a police officer.

I am sure this man has done many times to others what he did to me, and will do it again even more uninhibitedly, as his confidence was boosted by the encounter tonight. To people like him, the exhilaration they experience from bullying and intimidating the "socially inferior" and getting away with it is just too sweet to resist. It is as addictive as cocaine and heroin. For those who live at the bottom of society and labor hard from dawn to dusk to make ends meet, what options do they have when they are faced with bullies like that? They have no choice but to bite the bullet. This is the cold, hard fact of the mundane world we live in.

Civil Defense

This afternoon I got stranded in a traffic standstill at Suntec City.

Traffic is always messy at Suntec City. First, there is this big roundabout that loops around the Fountain of Wealth, where cars, taxis and buses coming and going in all directions converge, each pushing its own way through in the absence of traffic control signals. Second, this area is practically a "traffic trap", easy to enter but dreadful to exit. Two highways, the ECP and Nicoll Highway, provide fast and convenient access for incoming traffic. The outgoing traffic, however, has to depend largely on the narrow Temasek Avenue which takes motorists for a lengthy detour before reaching the main roads. I always think of this place as a traffic planner's big blunder.

And this was certainly not helped by someone's brilliant idea of shutting down one of the lanes of Temasek Avenue with some roadside construction.

With only one lane left passable on Temasek Avenue, the traffic in the whole area had effectively come to a standstill. Cars inched along between long intervals of complete stoppage. The greenhouse gas emissions from hundreds of idling vehicles were mixed with an air of

119

anxiety and desperation radiating from the people sitting inside them, filling the Saturday afternoon sky.

At a time like this, everybody's patience was hanging by a thread.

It took me a while just to traverse half of the roundabout to reach Temasek Avenue. While making the turn, I steered to take the lane on the right side, which was not blocked by the construction site some distance ahead. Since there was not enough space to straighten the car in the lane, my taxi was momentarily stuck in a diagonal position across two lanes. For that, I was rewarded with a long, angry beep from the car right behind, a black Honda Civic that looked old enough to have lived since the last millennium. It made me nervous but I tried to ignore it. As soon as space permitted, I straightened my car.

I turned on the radio to kill time. The "LTA traffic news" was being broadcast. The man on the radio said there was an accident somewhere on a highway and advised motorists to "avoid lane 1", and there was roadwork going on somewhere else, so "please avoid lane 2", and so on. I could never figure out why they have to give such advice. "Please avoid lane 1?" Isn't that *totally* obvious and unnecessary? Whenever I hear or see something like that, I feel frustrated at not being able to grasp the rationale or logic of it. Nonetheless, it didn't escape my notice that there was no mention of the traffic mess at Suntec City, the one I was painfully experiencing right now.

The car on my tail, the Civic, honked again. This time it was to get my attention. I peeked in the mirror and caught the driver showing me his middle finger. Staring in my direction, his eyeballs looked ready to pop out. "What is your problem?" I murmured. Again, I looked away. But I felt a knot form in my stomach.

We were still not moving. And then another honk. I turned my head around. The Honda driver was making hand signals to me and the message was crystal clear:

"Come out of your car and let's fight!"

I quickly turned my head back while waving my hand in dismissal. Crazy guy, I heard myself saying. I decided to ignore him, and hoped he would soon wear himself out and leave me alone.

To my astonishment, the man got out of his car and walked towards me!

I swore loudly. A confrontation was now inevitable.

He came to my side and glared at me with his body trembling in anger. He looked like an enraged black bear on the attack, bent on eating me alive.

He was bigger than I thought. Probably in his early thirties, he was of medium height but had a strong build, wearing a pair of faded jeans and a black T-shirt, which seemed to be on the verge of being burst open by his muscular body. His hands were clenched in tight fists and his upper arms were covered with tattoos of what seemed to be characters from Japanese comic books. His face was dotted with acne scars, his eyes burning with fire. He was a fierce man on all counts.

The danger was one hundred percent real. Unlike the lunatic who bullied me last night, this man was a "silver blade made of steel".

A Tamahagane steel!

While my mind raced madly for possible ways to avert what could mount to a life-threatening situation, my hand involuntarily lowered the window in a slow motion. I sensed that he was going to smash it with his fist if I didn't. I was expecting a blow to my face now. I took off my spectacles, and held his stare and waited.

He hesitated, and stood there staring at me, his fists opening and closing several times. Then he said through his teeth, "I feel like punch you in the face."

On that, I saw a slim chance of getting out of this grave danger in one piece. I knew the only way to do that was to talk him out of his anger, to be civil with him.

"Why?" I said as calmly as I could. "I didn't do anything to you."

"I just feel like punch you," the man said again, his eyes still deadly fixed on mine. The flame in his eyes, however, seemed to be shrinking a bit. Or maybe it was my imagination.

"I don't know why you are angry with me," I said. "I am just driving my taxi and that's all. I didn't do anything wrong."

At this time, another man walked over from their car. He came out from the passenger side. He was short and thin, and a few years younger. He wore a T-shirt with a picture of a ferocious Transformer robot on it, which compensated for his superficial frailty to some extent.

He, however, proved to be much fiercer than he looked. If the other guy was like a bear, this one was a certifiable hyena. He wedged himself between the muscle man and me, leaned to get close to my face, and shouted, "You shit! You piece of shit! The way you drive, we all saw it! Take two lanes same time! You shit!"

He was showering my face with his saliva. He also made a posture as if he were going to hit me.

"This is a traffic jam." Again, I had no choice but to be calm and civil. "You can't go anywhere anyway. So try to be patient, okay?"

"I don't have patience!" the small man shouted. But he stopped waving his fist in my face. He stood straight up and put his hands on his hips, looking like a replica of the robot on his shirt, equally furious and equally comical.

Up to this point, the traffic had remained at a standstill. But now it began to move slightly. When they saw the car in front of me had moved a distance of two cars' lengths, they were itchy to return to theirs.

"This is your lucky day," the big man said as he nudged his companion towards their car. "Your *fucking* lucky day."

During all this time as the drama unfolded, people in the surrounding cars were watching us with intense interest. I guess some of them might even have felt a little disappointed that it ended undramatically. But unaware to them, they served as my defense line and likely helped to prevent a dramatic outcome.

As the Chinese saying goes, "祸不单行" (bad things always come in multiples). Last night I had the misfortune of meeting a maniac who proved his superiority by yelling abusive words at me, and I let him get away as I lacked a witness. Today I just escaped by a hair's breadth from what could have been a nasty, nightmarish experience. Apart from my "civil defense" strategy, an important factor in the turnaround in today's event is the presence of witnesses, which would have made the husky man think twice before he swung his fist at me. Even if they did harm me, at least they wouldn't get away with it. With witnesses present, I could count on our system to protect me, to uphold justice for me. This is the difference between the events of today and yesterday.

May   2009

26

Tuesday

An Eighty Year Old Lady

It had been an hour and a half since midnight. My ambition to land at least one job with a midnight surcharge before going home was now in full retreat. I had been cruising nonstop around the CBD, passing through all the major nightspots. No luck. Tuesdays are always the slowest day of the week. I decided to call it a day.

On my way home I stopped at a 7-Eleven store on McCallum Street to get some cigarettes. Next to the store's entrance, in the shadow of the sidewalk, I noticed an old woman lying on the ground under the shelter of the arcade. She was resting on some partially flattened cardboard boxes and looked sound asleep. Scattered around her were more empty boxes in various sizes, along with a small rundown flatbed trolley. I paused for a moment in my tracks, wondering if she was ill or in need of help, but was hesitant to disturb her.

After I came out of the store I saw two young ladies standing in front of the old woman talking to her. She was now awake and sitting up against a pile of boxes. One of the girls held a blanket in her hand. They were talking gingerly to the old woman, apparently trying to give her the blanket. The old lady seemed too tired to respond, other than mumbling something in a weak voice.

I moved closer, stood next to the girls, and heard the old woman saying in Mandarin, "I was too tired. I fell asleep without knowing it. I will be going very soon." She said it apologetically, as if confessing something she had done wrong.

"Can you speak Chinese?" One of the girls turned to me and asked. I said yes. She asked me to tell the woman that this blanket was for her. I did so, but she didn't seem to have heard me. She responded, "I am tired and have to have a rest before I can get up and get going again."

I said to the girls that she appeared to have a hearing problem, and had probably mistaken us for someone who wanted to chase her away. One of the girls stepped close to the woman and laid the blanket gently on her legs and said, "This is for you." They left after that.

Both girls were locals and looked to be in their mid-twenties. The blanket they left for the old woman was brand new. They must have bought it just now in the 7-Eleven after they saw the lady sleeping on the ground. Their generosity and caring spirit made me feel a little guilty.

I decided to stay a while longer to see if I could convince the old lady to let me drive her home, as she had said she was too tired to move.

She was in her seventies at least, wearing a grey shirt and a pair of pants in a darker color. Both were badly wrinkled and dusted with dirt. Though she looked slightly better than a few moments ago, and her voice a bit louder and clearer, she remained weak. Her hearing was seriously impaired and despite my repeated attempts to speak to her, she didn't respond as if she understood me.

She, however, was in a mood to talk. She first lifted the blanket from her leg and said to me, "They are so kind. I don't need this. It will get dirty here." She placed it carefully on top of a carton box. Then she motioned me to sit down near her, and pulled up her pants to expose the lower part of her legs from ankle to knee. The appearance of her legs astonished me. They were like thin, dead tree trunks. They had a rugged surface and were black in color. While pressing her legs with a finger at random spots, she carried on nonchalantly, "My legs no good anymore. I get tired easily. My legs used to be red, you know, like chili pepper. After the doctors did operations on me, they became totally black. I was in hospital three times. One time I stayed in bed for three weeks and never came down. My hands, too, you see. Three of the fingers in each hand are frozen. Cannot use anymore. Only this two (thumb and index) can move. I can't comb my hair. Can't use chopsticks also."

At this moment, a man emerged from a narrow alley next to the 7-Eleven store. He was in his late thirties and had a bicycle with him. He was here for the old lady. He shot me an inquisitive look as he said something to the lady in a raised voice. The lady opened a styrofoam box next to her and took out a plastic bag containing a few empty bottles and some other containers and handed them to him.

I was glad to see the man as I had not been able to communicate with the old lady. I first put him at ease by saying I was just a taxi driver trying to see if the lady needed any help. I told him I wanted to give her a ride home but could not get her to understand me. He said she could not hear properly and would not be going home tonight because she needed to go some place nearby tomorrow morning to collect discarded boxes. I asked if he was related to her and he said he was not, but added that he had been helping her for the past fifteen years.

"Does she have any children?" I asked.

"Yes. She has two sons and a daughter," he answered. "I have met them."

"Do they take care of their mother?"

He shook his head and said nothing. He then told me that every day for the past fifteen years, he would come to the old lady twice a day. Once in the middle of the night to check on her and collect the bag of bottles, and again before eight in the morning to bring her food and water, and help her cut the boxes, load them on the trolley, and bring them to the recycling center to exchange for money, *fifty kilograms for $2*. She used to carry fifty kilograms herself, but not anymore. She was over eighty years old and her legs had some lymphatic vessel problems.

"Now is almost two, so I only sleep a few hours a day. I have my own job to do in Bukit Merah during the day. I have to go now." He put the plastic bag inside a basket mounted on his bicycle, said goodbye to me, and left.

After he was gone, the lady patted the styrofoam box at her side and said, "My ice are all gone now. I have to drink cold water. I get fire in my chest if I don't. Burning hot. Drives me crazy. I have to drink ice cold water to stay alive. Every day he fills the bottles with water and brings to me with some ice. I keep them in this box. Now, no more."

"You give me a minute," I said. I went to 7-Eleven and came back with an ice cold bottle of fruit drink. The lady took it, held it to her chest, and thanked me. She said, "Some people think I am too fussy, you know, having to drink cold water. They don't know I have no choice. It's burning inside here."

I took out $10, put it on her legs and said, "Here is some more money. You can buy more cold drinks after you finish this one." She didn't hear what I said but she understood. She took the money and said thank you again.

I left after that. It was past two already. I made a mental note to come back here tomorrow to check on the old lady again.

I went home via New Bridge Road. The street was empty, with only a few cars and taxis parked along the curb in front of some restaurants that were open all night long. I started to accelerate.

Suddenly, before the Cantonment Road junction, a man leapt out of the darkness and ran into the middle of the road with his arm extended, forcing me to stop abruptly. It was a white man in his forties and he told me to go to Pandan Valley via Grange Road.

I gritted my teeth and drove silently towards Pandan Valley. Privately, I was annoyed with him for jumping on the road like that. I almost hit him! But then again, had he stayed off the road, I would probably have missed him.

When we reached his place, the meter fare was $8. With the midnight surcharge, the total was $12 exactly.

Rather than feeling pleased that I had finally accomplished my initial goal, I felt eerie. This was exactly what I had given to the old lady just a moment ago!

The Game Plan

(1)

Around seven o'clock in the evening, two men and a woman boarded my taxi on Orchard Road. One of the men sat in the front seat and told me in Mandarin to go to a Lorong in Geylang. The woman pinpointed their destination with more specifics. "You know the frog porridge coffee shop there? That's the place." I said okay.

They were in their thirties and their accents indicated they were from China. The two in the back engaged in small talk and were clearly intimately related by the way they spoke to each other. The man sitting next to me was quiet and aloof, and kept his eyes gazing vacantly into the distance.

A phone rang. The woman answered the call. She um-ed to the caller several times and said in Mandarin that she would call back in a few minutes. She flipped the phone close and told the man beside her that the game was on. But instead of 20/40, which was initially suggested by her, the other party wanted to raise it to 30/60.

"If they like to play big," the man said, growing annoyed, "tell them let's just cut to the chase and do 50/100!"

"No. That's not a good idea," the woman said in an undertone. "We don't know them well. Let's do it their way today. 30/60. Plus, you know, it hasn't really been great for us lately. Our men brought in $2,000 the day before yesterday but lost more than $3,000 last night."

"I told you they must be replaced every two hours!" the man said with a raised voice.

"I know. I did that. I always do what you say," the woman said calmly, maintaining an air of grace.

The man loosened up a little, and asked in a softer tone, "How much you got with you?"

"$600 only."

"I will have someone bring $10,000 to you later." The man had set his seal of approval on the game plan.

The lady made the call and confirmed the game at ten o'clock.

That was when we reached the coffee shop.

(2)

Around 2am, I passed by the McCallum Street/Telok Ayer area and saw the eighty year old lady again. Although I had come here every day around this time to look for her since I met her a week ago, this was the only time we crossed paths. I was glad to see her in a much better shape this time. She must have had a good rest since she looked quite energetic. She was pushing her trolley down Amoy Street, a full load of tin containers piled on it.

When I pulled over by her side, she recognized me and said joyously, "Hey, boss." I knew about her hearing problem but nonetheless said to her, "How are you?"

She pointed to the stuff on her trolley and said, "I collect these today. Tomorrow I will do cardboard boxes again." I glanced at her harvest. They were all cooking oil containers, which she must have found from the dump site of the Telok Ayer Food Center nearby. But she didn't seem to want to spend much time talking with me today. She had work to do. Without another word, she started to look through a row of garbage cans, which had been left on the roadside by shopkeepers.

I stopped my car behind her. I had bought a bag of apples and oranges for her from a wet market two days ago but could not find her the previous two nights. I had kept the bag in the trunk. I went to check – they were still good, as shiny as the day I bought them. I took out the bag and went to her. She said she liked apples but one was enough. I said take them all, they could stay fresh for another couple of days. I put the bag on her trolley, said goodbye to her, and left.

Jun 2009
5
Friday

Shallow Dent, Deep Impression

Prior to signing the contract with the taxi company three months ago, I had indicated to them that I planned to take a trip to China in June with my family. This is something we do every year, I said. The sales manager, eager to get me on board, quickly obtained an approval from the management to grant me a temporary return of the taxi for ten days. Today was the day for the return.

Coincidentally, I was also invited by the company to attend a dialog session this morning so I was going there to kill two birds with one stone. The meeting was scheduled for 10:30am.

I arrived at the company before ten as I first wanted to take care of the taxi return. I filled out some forms as part of the procedure. Then I was told that the car had to be checked by the workshop. Since this would take some time, they asked me to attend the meeting first and come to sign the handover sheet later.

The dialog session was attended by ten or so taxi drivers. From the attendance form, I noticed that only half the names on the list had bothered to show up. The company had four representatives present.

I learned in the meeting that not all drivers were doing as badly as myself. Some of them benefited handsomely from the Corporate Drivers Program, an exclusive club of drivers who could obtain on-call jobs from contracted corporations like companies and hotels. To join the club you had to pay a monthly fee and buy a special dispatching device from the organizers of the club. The reason for the exclusivity, I gathered, was that the organizers, shrewd and business-minded taxi drivers themselves, were responsible for soliciting the corporate partners into the program using the company's name. How they divide, if they do, the membership fees between the company and the organizers was a mystery to me. Nevertheless, someone claimed during the meeting that as a newcomer to the club he had not been fairly treated, citing examples of odd hour or not-so-lucrative jobs that were given to him.

It was clear, however, that most of the drivers were, like myself, doing poorly on the roads. They never got any calls from the company's dispatch center and the competition on the streets was cut-throat. The united message from all the drivers present at the meeting was that the company should do more to alleviate our burden.

During the meeting, the company representatives presented some new marketing schemes aimed at increasing taxi ridership. In my opinion it was too insignificant to have any impact.

After the meeting, I went to the workshop to finish what I expected to be nothing more than a mere formality – signing the handover paper. To my surprise I was told by a mechanic that they had found two body damages on the car, for which I had to pay $160 for the repair.

"How could that be possible?" I said in disbelief.

He showed me the work sheet. One of the "damages" was located on the driver's door, and was marked "$100" for repair. I went to the car to check. "It was dented by a car parked next to yours when its door is opened," the mechanic said as he pointed the dent to me.

The dent was so tiny that it was practically invisible if you didn't know where to look. It was only about half an inch in length and was so shallow you had to put your finger there to feel the unevenness. It was difficult to see not only because of its size, but also because the car was covered with advertisement stickers that masked it.

"And you want to charge me $100 for this?" I turned to him and asked.

"Standard procedure," he answered, looking at his sheet.

"This is just unbelievable." I shook my head in dismay. "This doesn't make any sense. When the car was issued to me three months ago, nobody went through its body condition with me in this much detail. I am not talking about mopping over it with my bare hands, you know, which is exactly what I think will be needed to spot a dent like that. No. I only mean in reasonable detail, like standing on each side and scanning it with a reasonable amount of time. No! Never! I was only led by somebody to walk around it for a few seconds! That's how its condition was checked last time! How would I possibly know this wasn't there at the time when the car was given to me?"

The man found it difficult to quash my argument. Ironically, he was the same man who handled the handover procedure with me three months earlier. He knew how it was done. He paused for a moment and said to me, "Okay. I will talk to my supervisor to strike these charges." Then, he crossed out both damages on my handover sheet with a pen and gave it to me for my signature. He didn't bother to show me the other damaged site, which I assumed was even more negligible.

I signed the sheet, thanked him, and left.

I was thinking about what happened in the workshop on the MRT on my way home. I toyed with the possibility that this might be some kind of scam to cheat submissive drivers. If I had not protested, I would have been $160 poorer. It was plausible that even if I paid up, the dent might have been left unrepaired.

But usually I prefer to take things at their face value whenever possible. I would rather believe this was an honest, isolated incident. If so, I had to applaud the skill and the professionalism of the mechanic for spotting the tiny dent on the car, and his kind consideration to waive the cost of the repair for me.

Nevertheless, even if the dent was my fault, I still found the $100 charge for a minor mark on an old rundown taxi incredibly thick-skinned. Then again, corporations are nothing if not greedy. However extraordinary it looked to me, it was just a "standard procedure", and the way of everyday capitalism.

Half A Tank Of Diesel

This morning I stopped at a red light on Depot Road. A man stood at the roadside some twenty meters ahead with his arm in the air, wanting to hire my taxi. As I waited for the light to turn green, a red TransCab taxi which had stopped across the junction in the opposite direction suddenly made a U-turn in the face of a red light to pick up the man. I had customers grabbed from me by other taxis many times before, but this was the first time someone did that by running a red light.

In an article published in The Straits Times less than two weeks ago (June 6, 2009), it was reported that the taxi ridership in Singapore in the first quarter of the year had dropped to a five year low. A sixty-two year old taxi driver named Mr. Yeow, who had been driving for more than twenty years, told the reporter that he pocketed $30 to $40 a day after deducting costs, down from $50 to $60 a year ago. I found his numbers believable as they matched well with mine. Therefore, I didn't blame the TransCab driver for doing anything he could to seize an earning opportunity.

What the driver didn't know was that he didn't have to break the law to get his customer this time, as I was not going to take any passengers this morning. I was on my way to the company workshop to have the car serviced, and was already late.

I also had another issue I wanted to resolve with the company today.

I came back from my trip to China last Saturday. On Monday, the day before yesterday, I went to the company to reclaim my taxi. The good news was that they didn't mention the $160 damage repair charge when they checked my account for outstanding fees before they released the car to me. So it had indeed been struck off. The bad news was that after I got the car back, I found all the personal stuff I left in the car missing, including some CDs, a street directory, and some unused notebooks and pens. Also gone was half a tank of diesel.

I would have let it go had I not realized somebody had driven the taxi in my absence to pick up customers, with free diesel courtesy of me! I didn't know exactly how much this person had made because I didn't clear my record in the meter before I left, so his earnings were mixed up with mine. I also forgot to record the mileage before I returned the car. But one thing was certain – he had made at least one trip with a fare of $12.20, as this amount was paid by credit card. In my entire taxi career, I had never taken a single payment by credit card as I didn't know how to and never bothered to learn. I called the company customer service yesterday to report this finding and was told they would investigate. Today, I came to check this out.

The young lady who received me at the service counter told me they could not locate my belongings. Neither had they been able to find out who had driven my taxi.

"Did the workshop people know this taxi is returned on a temporary basis, and will be reclaimed by the same driver after ten days?" I asked her.

"Yes, they know," she said. "It's in the computer."

I said in that case, I didn't understand why they cleared my personal stuff from the car. But more importantly, it was not right to let somebody drive it and make money at my expense. "I paid for the diesel," I said.

The girl didn't know what to say. She knew I had hard evidence. A lady in her late thirties, who looked like a manager and had been standing behind the girl listening to our conversation, stepped forward at this time and said, "The company has the right to relocate the taxi to other drivers as it sees fit."

"If you say so," I said, looking into her eyes. "But who is this person you relocated my taxi to? I would like to talk to him. I would want compensation from him for my fuel."

"Did you record your level of fuels at the time you returned your taxi?" The lady challenged me in a hostile tone. "Who is there to confirm your statement that you had left with half a tank of diesel? How do we know it wasn't already empty when you returned the car?"

"Get real," I said scornfully. "I have to cross the whole country to come to this place. Do you think I would risk breaking down halfway by driving with an empty tank?"

"Even so," she said, "the fuel may have been consumed by testing in the workshop."

"How do you explain, then, the $12.20 credit card payment?" I asked.

"That could be a test for credit card machine as well," she said.

"Then why bother $12.20? Why not something more straightforward, like $10, or $20? Do you think you are making any sense yourself?" I stood up and raised my voice. "I demand a thorough investigation of this matter and I want a truthful explanation in writing. Until then, I will not let this matter be brushed aside by you or anybody else. Watch me if you don't believe me."

I was going to storm out of the lobby when somebody approached me. He was the sales manager who first persuaded me to sign up with the company. He also arranged the temporary taxi return for me. "Mr. Cai," he said with a smile, "how about we solve this issue here once and for all?"

"How?" I stopped in my tracks and rolled my eyes at him.

"Would you accept two sets of seat cushions for the loss of your fuel and other belongings?" he asked.

I looked at him wordlessly for a moment. He earned my respect. He must have noticed the bath towel I was holding, and guessed correctly about its sweat-absorbing function. I had taken the towel from the driver's seat as I left the car for servicing in the workshop, and rolled it into a cylinder and held it under my arm while I was talking with the ladies. He was the nicest guy I knew in this company. Now, maybe he was also the smartest.

Finally, I said softly, "Okay, and thanks for your help."

Jun 2009
20
Saturday

Three Chinese Students/Bar Girls

This evening four young people, three girls and one boy, flagged down my taxi at the Maxwell Food Center and told me to go to Clarke Quay.

They were part of a larger group on their way to a farewell party held for a girl friend who was returning to China, her home country, in the coming days. The rest of the entourage had left a moment ago.

They were all students from China, in their late teens to early twenties. On the way, most of their conversation revolved around their experiences as bar girls. Whatever they were supposed to study here, or their families back in China thought they studied here, didn't take up much of their time. One girl said she only had two hours of school each day, and the other one said she had three. All three girls had worked in bars, clubs or karaoke lounges.

One girl said she worked for $8 an hour in a bar sometime ago. The other one said this was unusually high, since she was only paid $5 per hour at the place she worked. "At first, everything in the pub looked normal," she recounted. "But after some time, as our salaries accumulated to $200, the boss withheld the money and began to make us do 'that thing'. If we refused to go out with customers who had that 'special request', the boss said we would never see the money."

"What would you do then?" the boy who sat in the front seat asked.

"What else can we do?" the girl said matter-of-factly. "We either had to do what he wanted us to do, or quit the job without getting the money back. To me, $200 is still a lot of money."

She didn't say what she chose to do.

"You shouldn't be working in these places," the boy said. He was a little upset now. "Why don't you find something else to do?"

"Like what?" one of the girls replied. "We can't work in McDonalds, 7-Eleven, or any other places that require a work permit."

All the girls were young and good looking. Though they appeared content, even happy, with what they did in their spare time, I am sure their parents would be badly hurt if they knew what their daughters were really up to here in Singapore.

To me, this was nothing new. I already knew that girls from China had become the cornerstone of the night entertainment industry here. If you drove a taxi, you would know too.

A White Gentleman

"Are we taking a taxi?" I heard a lady say in a Singlish accent.

"Yes," a man replied.

"But it is so close," the lady said again. "We can walk there in five minutes."

The door opened. A white man and an Asian woman came in to the back seat.

"I am too tired to walk," the man said to her. He handed me a currency note and said, "Five dollars to take us to Amara Hotel. No need to switch on the meter."

He then pulled the lady into his arms and kissed her for a long moment. Realizing the car had not moved, the white man looked up at me and said, "Please go. What are you waiting for?"

"This is a fifty," I said, holding up the money.

"It is? Oh." He grabbed the money back. He fished in his pocket for a moment and found another note. "For your honesty, I am doubling my offer. Ten dollars to Amara hotel." I took the money and started the car.

They boarded my taxi in front of the M Hotel on Anson Road, which is only a block away from the Amara Hotel. I didn't have a good look at them before they came in, but from my glimpses in the mirror, the white man was quite tall and probably in his thirties, whereas the Asian woman was likely a local in her mid twenties, slim, long-haired, sexily dressed. They had probably come from a bar in the hotel as they reeked of alcohol. It was half past midnight.

They kissed again. The girl said, "It's too early to go to bed now. I feel like go dancing. Can we go dancing please?"

"Okay. Where do you want to go?" the man asked.

"Hmmm. How about Saint James? It's not far from here," the girl said. "Come on. Let's go."

I was all ears, prepared to change course if the man said yes.

For some reason, the man suddenly seemed to have lost his appetite. "You know what? I am really tired, actually. I want to go back to hotel. But, if you really want to, you can go by all means," he said.

"I want to go," the girl said stubbornly.

"Fine." The man leaned forward and said to me. "You drop me off at Amara and take the lady to Saint James. You can start the meter from the Amara Hotel. Okay?"

I said okay.

We were at the Amara Hotel now, but the man was not getting out yet, as the lady had become unhappy. He whispered something in her ear. The woman was quiet for a while and then they started to get out together. The man said sorry to me for changing the plan.

I had no idea what the relationship between this couple was. Maybe it was a one night stand, or maybe it wasn't. But generally speaking, I have seen many local girls going out with white men. The official figures also showed a palpable increase in interracial marriages in Singapore. And I believe this trend is going to continue in the future.

Poison In Disguise

Some twenty minutes before midnight, I was cooling my heels at the taxi stand next to Cuppage Plaza. Normally business was good at this place, but today it was unusually quiet.

Finally, someone came in. It was a Chinese lady, and she told me in Mandarin to go to Balestier Road.

I had taken passengers from Orchard to Balestier many times in the past. I normally go either via Cavenagh Road/ Kampong Java/Thomson Road, or by CTE/Moulmein Road, depending on which end of Balestier the destinations were closer to. Today, without thinking, I took the former route.

As I turned onto Cavenagh Road the lady said, "Why didn't you go by CTE?"

"Oh, sorry," I replied, looking at her in the mirror. "I didn't ask you which way you want me to take. But there shouldn't be much of difference. We can get there quickly by this way also."

But she was unforgiving. "You don't need me to tell you how to go. You are the taxi driver and you should know which way is the best way," she said.

In a situation like this, I employed my stock answer:

"Sorry for that. Later you can pay me whatever you want to pay. Okay?"

She didn't respond.

She was in her early thirties. She spoke Mandarin with a northern accent. The fact she did not speak English when she first spoke to me suggested she probably did not know any. From the way she was dressed she didn't look to be one of the Chinese girls working in the night entertainment industry.

Her place was near the end of Moulmein Road. This meant that I had indeed made a mistake. When we stopped at her destination, the meter fare was $7.

"I take taxi every day," she said. "The fare is always $5."

"$5 is fine. No problem." I was eager to minimize her unhappiness. "You can just pay me $5."

She gave me a $5 note, but then said, "I can pay you $7 if you give me a receipt."

"I'll just take $5," I said to her, feeling grateful for her generosity. "Don't worry about the meter. If you want a receipt, however, I can give you one regardless." I thought maybe she needed a receipt to claim the expense.

She thought about it for a moment and said, "I want a receipt and I will pay $7."

"Okay, if that's what you want," I said. I printed out the receipt and gave it to her. She handed me a $2 note. I thanked her and took the money.

She opened the door. With one leg out, she suddenly said in a venomous tone, "*I will file a complaint on you!*"

With that she got out and slammed the door.

I was completely stunned.

Two Men At Bus Stops

(1)

In the late evening, around 10:30pm, I was on my way back from Upper Bukit Timah. I turned from Dunearn Road to Farrer Road and headed towards Queenstown.

Soon after I got on Farrer Road, a lone man sitting at a bus stop stood up and flagged me down. He came in and took the back seat and told me in Hokkien to take him to Clementi.

He was a local Chinese in his mid-fifties. He wore a blue striped polo shirt and a pair of pants in a dark color; both looked sloppy and worn out. On his face was an expression of fatigue and impatience. He must have just gotten off work, or had been waiting at the bus stop for a long time.

As I drove along, I asked him in Mandarin, "Where in Clementi do you want to go?"

"You just go straight and I'll let you know later," he answered impatiently, again in Hokkien.

My knowledge of Hokkien was very limited and I was afraid I might not be able to understand him if he gave me instructions later in this dialect. So I looked at him in the mirror and said apologetically, "Sorry, could you please speak Mandarin or English? I am not very good at Hokkien."

"Stop, stop," he said suddenly in English.

I immediately stopped. I turned my head to see what was wrong.

To my surprise, he opened the door and began to get out. He stood outside the car, holding the door open, and shouted at me angrily in English, "I am the one with money! I don't have to listen to you! There're as many taxis on the roads as the ants on the ground. Why I have to take shit from you?" With that, he slammed the door shut.

As he moved away from my car towards another taxi coming in our direction, I watched him in total bewilderment. What did I say? Why was he so offended by my harmless request? After all, he could speak English very well. How could he do this to me?

I looked at the meter. It showed $3.60. I thought about whether I should try to make him pay but decided to let it go. I turned the meter off and drove away.

In retrospect, I don't blame him for what he did. He was probably so stressed out by other things in life that he wanted to take it out on someone when he had a chance. Who would be an easier target than a cabdriver who speaks *Chinese* Chinese?

(2)

At two in the morning, on one of the inner streets of Ang Mo Kio, I dropped off what I decided would be my last customer of the day. I killed the engine at a bus stop and came out to catch a breeze and a smoke.

The street was quiet and motionless, except for a man enjoying himself about ten to fifteen meters away from me on the pavement. He was in his fifties or sixties, judging from the thin grey hair on his head and the thick lines on his face, but had the physique of a thirty or forty year old. He was practicing kung fu stunts. With a long stick in his hand, he moved briskly back and forth, swinging the stick around his body, fending off imaginary enemies like a kung fu master from an old Jackie Chan movie. I watched him in amazement.

Even though I was his sole audience, my presence encouraged him. He steadily increased the speed and sophistication of his movements. In what appeared to be his final act, he spun himself with the stick pressed to his waist for a few seconds before jumping up and striking the ground with the stick as he descended. He hit the ground so hard that the stick broke into two pieces.

Holding half a stick in his hand, he covered his embarrassment well with some tricky footwork and spun himself again. At the end of the spinning, he released the broken weapon in his hand, which flew high into the sky and dropped into a faraway ditch on the side of the street.

He let out a long breath and stood still for a few seconds before strolling towards me. He walked past me and lay down on a bench under the shelter of the bus stop. With eyes closed and hands clasped under his head, he seemed to have decided to spend the night there. For the rest of the time I stayed, I didn't detect the slightest hint of movement from him.

I left a few minutes after that.

$3 CBD Surcharge

Ten minutes after 5pm, a tall Caucasian man in his early forties boarded my taxi at the Telok Ayer taxi stand and told me to go to a place in the River Valley area. As I negotiated the main traffic on Cross Street, I said to him that there would be a $3 surcharge for this trip on the top of the meter fare. He shot a glance at the meter and muttered, "We'll see about that."

"What the heck does that mean?" I thought, but I didn't say anything.

When I stopped in front of a shophouse at the end of the trip, the meter fare was $5.85. "Eight eighty-five," I announced to him. "Do you need a receipt?"

The white man gave me only $6. "Keep the change," he said as he opened the door.

"Wait." I turned to face him. "There is a $3 CBD surcharge. I told you already."

"Don't try to cheat me," he said, and stepped out, a scornful expression on his face.

"Hey! You wait!" I called after him. But he ignored me, quickly opened the door of the shophouse, and disappeared behind it. *You don't try to cheat me!* Angered by his remarks, I decided to go after him, confront him, and

149

make him apologize for what he just said to me. I moved the car closer to the curb, turned off the engine, and got out.

There was a shiny metal plaque affixed on the wall beside the door he entered. Etched on it was a name of a company. I was about to bang the door open when an LTA traffic warden on a motorbike came into view. He stopped about twenty or thirty meters away from me, and started checking for parking violations along the street, which was marked by a zigzag line. I didn't want to lose a watermelon while picking up a sesame seed (捡了芝麻丢了西瓜). A parking ticket would cost me $60, maybe more. Even a hard-won apology from that cocky white man wouldn't be worth that amount of money. So I thought I had better go buddy up with the LTA man first.

I approached the traffic warden, who was a young local in his twenties, and told him I had a Caucasian customer who refused to pay the CBD surcharge and I had to leave my taxi on the street in order to go after him. He replied, "No need to talk to him. Just call 999 and let the police deal with people like that."

"I want to see if I can solve this problem without the police," I said.

"Do you know where he went?" he asked.

"Yes. Into this shophouse," I said as I pointed to the building next to us.

"Okay. Go ahead," he said with a drop of authoritative flavor in his tone, "but don't take too long."

I opened the door and saw a single flight of stairs leading to two doors on the second floor. I went up and pushed open the first glass door on my left.

There he was.

The interior of the room had been renovated recently,

and had a modern yet cozy ambiance. The room was spacious and partitioned into two sections by a glass wall. The inner area by the window was smaller and was occupied by an oval-shaped, wooden table surrounded by several matching armchairs. The white man was sitting at the end of the table with two other men at his sides. One was an Asian and the other a Caucasian; both seemed junior in rank and younger in age. They were in a meeting.

The lights in the outer area were off so it was considerably darker than the brightly lit meeting room. The glass door to the meeting room was closed and none of them had noticed my intrusion. There was an unmanned reception desk near the front door. I hammered it loudly with my fist.

They looked up with a start. The tall white man instantly recognized me. With an expression of disbelief and dismay, he put down some papers on the table and said something to his colleagues, of which I could only vaguely make out the word "cabdriver". The younger white man in his thirties stood up and strode to my side, then grabbed my arm and attempted to shove me out the door while saying, "You shouldn't be here."

"Get off me!" I yanked my arm free. I pointed to the inner room and said curtly to the young man, "Your boss owes me money!"

He seemed unsure what to do with me now, and stood near the wall and rolled his eyes at the men inside, who were apparently discussing why a cabdriver had burst into their office uninvited. Then the Asian man stood up, walked to the window, and looked down at where my taxi was parked. He came back to the white man and said something. The white man reluctantly stood up and crossed over to face me.

151

"How much do I owe you?" he asked in a subdued voice, as he took his wallet out from his back pocket, his head bent and eyes downcast.

"Three dollars."

He took out two $2 notes and put them in my hand and said, "Here is four. Now can you please leave? We are having a meeting here."

I stared at him. He seemed embarrassed and avoided eye contact with me. My initial motive for coming up here, to demand an apology from him, had now evaporated. I swallowed the words on the tip of my tongue, turned and walked out.

As I came out of the building, the LTA man was still at his original spot, busy printing out a parking ticket. He saw me and raised his jaw at me. I gave him a thumbs-up signal. He gave one back.

I started my car and drove away.

Driving Miss Edgy

(1)

Late in the evening, a man and a lady flagged down my taxi outside a coffee shop in Geylang. After they settled in the back seat, the man asked me in Mandarin, "Do you know any Hotel 81 somewhere near but out of the Geylang area?"

Hotel 81 is the McDonald's of the hotel industry in Singapore. Its growth in recent years has been particularly impressive. The budget hotel chain now has outlets all over the island. Apparently, there has been a rapid increase in the demand for cheaper hotels in Singapore, an intriguing phenomenon. As these hotels are unlikely the accommodation of choice for travelers from developed countries, the surging demand must reflect a booming trend of tourists from China and other developing countries in the region. But I am not sure that is the only reason.

"How about the ones on Lavender or Balestier? There are a few of them in that area," I answered.

"Okay. Lavender should be fine," the man said.

He was a local Chinese at least in his mid fifties. He was thin, of medium height, and carelessly dressed in a short sleeved shirt and long pants that looked like it had

153

been worn continuously for days and smelled of garlic-marinated chicken barbecued by cigarette smoke. He had been holding the hand of the lady since I saw them.

She was less than half his age, young enough to be his daughter. Taller than the old man by half a head, wearing shoulder-length hair and a long light blue dress, she could easily pass for a fashion model if she catwalked on Orchard Road. Right now she looked jittery, like a spooked rabbit who had just outrun a hungry wolf. Eyes flickering uneasily from side to side, she said, "Can we go as far as possible? The farther from Geylang, the better." Her accent was from the northern Chinese provinces.

The man patted her hand and said, "Lavender should be far enough. Don't worry."

"You don't know how tough they are," she said, apparently referring to the police. "They took away a friend of mine the other day at the coffee shop even though she had a return air ticket in her pocket."

"The police won't come this far. You can ask the uncle." The man was trying his best to calm her down. "Right, uncle?"

"Yeah, I think so. The police won't come this way." I echoed his words, even though I had no idea if they were true. I said that because I didn't want to appear to be ripping them off by giving false suggestions.

"See? Just relax. Okay?" the man said in a reassuring voice.

When we stopped outside the hotel on Lavender Street, the girl was hesitant to get out. To her, the route seemed too short.

"This is it? No, this is no good," she said. "This is still too close to Geylang. I want to go farther away."

The man, on the other hand, had no intention of either

154

spending more money on the taxi fare or waiting any longer to get the girl to bed, or both. He said to her softly but with detectable impatience, "Don't worry. Here is very safe already. Come on. Let's get out."

Still, she made no movement. The man paid the fare despite her disapproval. He then started to drag the woman's arm to get her out of the car. She knew she had no choice now. She got out reluctantly. The man put his arm around her and half-pushed, half-carried her into the hotel's front door.

(2)

I drove another nervous lady a few hours later.

Around 2am on a small street in Chinatown, I saw a middle-aged woman and a man in his thirties standing in front of a shophouse. They flagged me down. The man opened the door to the back seat and ushered the lady into the car. He closed the door and came to my side and said, "Uncle, please take the lady to Tampines."

He waved goodbye to the lady and went back inside the house.

This place housed several private gambling clubs. I knew this because I had taken passengers from here before, and they were always middle-aged women. I remembered about two weeks ago, I picked up a lady from here who was friendly and talkative, joking about her recent spate of bad luck. She lightheartedly told me she had lost more than three thousand dollars in this place within a month.

But this lady sitting behind me now was quiet and edgy. She had not made herself comfortable in the back. Instead, she hunched over slightly, arms tightly crossed over a handbag she clutched to her chest, as if she was having a stomachache.

"Playing Mahjong all night?" I asked casually, trying to build a friendly atmosphere to help her loosen up.

"Yes," she answered reluctantly after a lag.

"How is your luck tonight?"

She didn't reply.

The coziness ended right there. I drove the rest of the trip in silence.

When we reached her place on Tampines Street xx, the fare was $19 something. She gave me $20. Then she took out a $2 note and said, "I give you two more dollars and you walk me to my block. Is it okay?"

I said sure. I wanted a smoke anyway.

I left the car at the side of the street and followed her to her block, which was about forty or fifty meters from the street. She was still holding her handbag against her chest as she walked. After we got there she said, "You stand here. My unit is up there. You see that window? You don't go away until I give you a signal from that window. Okay?"

"Fine," I said.

A few minutes later, she appeared from the window and waved to me. I turned and walked back to my car.

She must have won a lot of money tonight.

Discourteous Movement

Ever since the 1970s, Singapore has carried out a series of campaigns to promote social courtesy. After many years of earnest effort from the government, how effective have these campaigns been and what changes have they achieved? I don't know. But judging from what I see on the roads, I think they still leave much to be desired.

Tonight was an example. Sometime after midnight, I was on my way back to the city from Bedok. I stopped before a red light at an intersection on New Upper Changi Road. About twenty meters in front of me, a group of four people were standing by the roadside, waiting for a taxi.

I was the first car in the extreme left lane. There were two other taxis behind me. Standing nose-to-nose with me in the middle lane was a motorcycle, which was followed by a private car and yet another taxi. Further to the right, in the extreme right lane, was a blue Comfort Sonata. All five taxis had a green light on top, meaning they were hungry for passengers.

I sized up the situation while waiting for the signal to change. I was definitely in an advantageous position. The other taxis couldn't possibly take these people from me this time, except, perhaps, for the Sonata if it could go

157

supersonic. However, considering the short distance these people stood from my car, and the presence of a motorcycle in the middle lane which the Sonata would risk running over if its driver was insane enough to try to grab these passengers, I should be pretty safe.

But I was wrong.

Before the traffic light turned green, the Sonata in the far right lane was restless. It jerked forward inch by inch, like a racehorse impatiently waiting for the gate to pop open. It was clear that the Sonata driver was bent on grabbing this opportunity. Sure enough, as soon as the green light came up, the Sonata leaped into a full sprint and cut across three lanes to get in front of me before I could reach the other side of the intersection. The motorcyclist, who I had trusted to act as a shield for me, was smart enough to fathom the intention of the Sonata driver, and waited for the taxi to pass before roaring off.

Once again, I watched the Sonata pick up the passengers that should have been mine. I felt I was watching a roasted Peking duck slip off my plate and fly out the window.

That was the way my luck went nowadays.

A Comrade From The UK

A Caucasian couple in their thirties boarded my taxi at the Raffles City taxi stand around nine-thirty in the evening, and told me to take them to Clarke Quay. I looked at them in the mirror and said cautiously that there would be a $3 surcharge on top of the meter fare. The man gave me a disarming smile and said "that's fine," as if he was already familiar with the levy.

The CBD surcharge has given me more troubles than anything else during my taxi driving experience so far. Every time I pick up a passenger when the CBD surcharge is applicable, I dread the moment of telling/reminding him or her about it. More often than I would have expected, even the local passengers were not aware that this surcharge applied all the way to midnight, long after the ERP gantries are turned off. To many people this is absurd. It is therefore understandable for some of them to doubt my words, despite the sticker on the window specifying all the surcharges, albeit in fine print. Some would pick up the phone and call somebody to verify its truthfulness. Some, on rare occasions, simply refuse to pay.

I was just glad I didn't have to worry about it this time.

As it turned out, the man readily accepted the CBD surcharge not because of his prior knowledge about it. It was because of his comradely trust in a fellow taxi driver. He told me that he too drove a taxi for a living in the UK.

He and his wife were touring Singapore as part of their holiday in the Far East. Out of his professional curiosity, he asked me what other surcharges we have here in Singapore. I explained them to him as thoroughly as I could.

"Do you have troubles with your customers?" he asked.

"Of course. All the time," I said, tongue-in-cheek.

He laughed. "Me too. All the time."

His wife, a good-looking woman who had been quiet till now, was quick to attenuate the male habitual tendency to exaggerate. "Not all the time, dear."

He smiled at her and said good-naturedly, "You are right. Sometimes." He then said to me that most of his problems with passengers were alcohol related. In his home city, people liked to drink beers, which were cheap and abundant. "I have found the beers here are very expensive. Maybe you don't have so many drinking related problems as we do?"

"I am not sure how ours would compare with yours," I answered, "but you will be surprised to see how many people hanging out in bars and pubs at night in Singapore."

When we reached Clarke Quay, the total fare was $6.40 ($3.40 plus the CBD surcharge). The man took out a $10 note, and said something to his wife in an undertone. She nodded in response. He then handed the note to me and said, "Please keep the change. It's been very nice talking to you."

I was taken aback by their generosity. Gratefully, I thanked them as they stepped out.

The Unbearable Heaviness Of Being

Forty minutes into the evening peak hours, I was waiting at the Bukit Merah Central taxi stand.

Despite its proximity to Chinatown and the financial district, and its long history as the epicenter of one of the earliest housing estates in Singapore, Bukit Merah Central is far less glamorous than other regional centers. There are no modern attractions such as shopping malls, cinemas, restaurants, or disco pubs to draw the crowds. There used to be a public swimming complex next to the bus terminal, but it had been shut for many years. The only saving grace was an NTUC Fairprice supermarket, one of the largest in town.

I noticed an Indian woman walking slowly in my direction. She lumbered along, carrying several Fairprice grocery bags, her body tilting from side to side with each heavy step.

She finally reached my taxi and motioned me to open the trunk so she could place her bags inside. Then she came in, sat in the front seat and told me to go to Telok Blangah Way, a five to eight minutes drive depending on the traffic lights.

Although the short distance of the trip was a disappointment to me, it was expected. Most people taking taxis from here were residents of the neighboring HDB estates with too many grocery bags to go home by bus. My mind was occupied by something else. I glanced at her and asked, "What do you have in your bags?"

"What do you mean?" She looked at me as if she found my question rudely intrusive.

"Oh, nothing," I quickly explained. "I just want to say that if you have seafood in there, I'd like to put some newspaper underneath your bags, since I had some troublesome experience before..."

"No seafood." She cut me off. "Only fruits and vegetables."

I apologized for asking the question. She said it was okay, she understood my concern.

From close up, I realized she was younger than I thought when I saw her from a distance. She was probably in her late forties, and wore an oversized brown dress.

She turned to me and asked, "What about durian? You mind if I have durian?"

"No. Durian is ok," I said with a smile. "The smell of durian doesn't stay long."

"Yeah," she said. "Otherwise, how am I supposed to carry it? Buses don't allow it. MRT don't allow it. If taxis also don't allow it..."

"I am sure most taxis will allow it," I said.

Looking for something to say, I asked, "You are not working today?"

She gave me an "are you making fun of me?" kind of look and said, "You find me a job and I will work."

I felt stupid. I was quiet for a moment, trying to imagine

what other good-natured taxi uncles would do in this case. I then told her that if she was looking for a job she could look in the newspapers, talk to friends, or ask her MPs for help.

We were reaching her stop, which was in a carpark next to an HDB block. She took out her wallet, held it in her hand, and said slowly, "Yeah. But I have this arthritis for many years. I have never been in a working condition."

That was what caused her heavy steps, I realized.

I tried to cheer her up. "That's okay. You don't have to work then. At least you have your husband to support you."

"My husband passed away," she said under her breath. Her hands stopped opening her wallet.

I stuttered, "I…I'm sorry."

She looked at me, her eyes two ice cubes melting under the sun. "You know a month and half ago, in the news, a husband and a son jumped off a building…"

As if struck by lightning, I felt a current bolt from my scalp to my feet. "My god. That's your…" I froze in shock.

"Yes. That's my…husband and…my boy." Her tears finally overran the dam and streamed down her cheeks.

I read the news after I came back from the trip to China. This was one of the most heartbreaking family tragedies I had heard of in Singapore. I was extremely saddened by the realization that human lives were so fragile, and could be shattered at the most unexpected moments.

According to the reports, the sequence of events on June 6, 2009, were as follows:

That evening, twenty-five year old Raja was meeting with some of his friends near his residence. They had some drinks. He had been unhappy lately as he lost his job about

*a month ago. During the gathering, his younger brother
called and asked him to go somewhere else together, but
Raja said he was tired and didn't want to go.*

*Around 10:30pm, he was back home in his apartment
on the ninth floor, but not for long. He told his mother that
he was going out again. His mother was worried about him
as he looked a little tipsy and asked him to stay at home.
But he was in no mood to listen to her.*

*On his way out his father came to speak to him, saying
he should listen to his mother and not go out at this hour.
They got into a heated argument. His father said he should
worry about finding a job rather than hanging out aimlessly.
Raja was further upset by the remarks. He stepped out of
his house and locked the front gate from the outside with
a padlock.*

*He then walked to the edge of the corridor, said he
was not a worthy son to his parents and jumped over the
parapet in front of his family.*

*The family was locked inside and could do nothing
to stop him. They witnessed the tragedy in horror, and
immediately called their relatives and the police for help.*

*The police came and had to call the civil defense
personnel to cut the lock to free the family, who came out
to see Raja lying dead on the ground nine floors below.*

*The family collapsed in grief on the ground floor,
accompanied by their relatives and the police. They were
then led to a nearby bench to sit and calm down. After a
while, the father left and before anyone became aware of
his movements, he took the lift to the tenth floor. He jumped
off the building crying "my son!" and landed on the ground
next to his son's body.*

*Both father and son were pronounced dead at the
scene.*

164

"My boy," the woman wiped some tears and said, "I loved him. I loved him so much. Every time he couldn't sleep at night he asked me, mama, come here. I came to sit by him, put my hand here, where his heart was beating. He would fall asleep right away." She put her hand over her heart to demonstrate.

She slowly turned her head, and pointed to the cement ground along the side of the building. "That's where my son was, and that's where my husband was."

I stared at the ground. Cold, hard cement, only a few steps away from my car. On the surface, any trace of blood from the two people she loved most had long been washed away. But I was certain, deep in the heart of the soil, their blood was still there, and would stay there forever.

"Sometimes I tell myself," she said, her eyes staring blankly ahead, "at least they are together up there, taking care of each other."

I looked at the woman. Her face was still covered with tears. Could anybody in this world possibly know what she had gone through? Only a short while ago, I was worried about her bags contaminating my taxi... I bit my lip and struggled to contain my own tears.

"I have to go on with my life. I have two other children to take care of," she said as she opened her wallet. I pressed my hand on hers and said in a shivering voice, "I can't take money from you."

"You can. Business is business," she insisted.

"No. I really can't." That was the only thing I could say.

"Please. Even if just a little bit," she said as she took out some money from her wallet. "It will make me feel better."

Her wallet was thin and empty. I could see there were

only three or four $2 notes inside. She took out two of them and put them in my hand. She looked into my eyes and said, "You understand me?"

The $4 she gave me was not "just a little bit". It was almost the full fare, but I couldn't speak. I just nodded.

She got out, took the bags, and walked slowly towards the building, shifting her weight from side to side, passing by the spots where her son and husband landed a month and a half ago.

With her heavy steps…

A note of explanation: It has been a general rule that my stories do not contain information which would allow the identification of persons involved in the events described. This story is an exception as it was about a tragic event that had already been made public by the news media.

Epilogue

To see a world in a grain of sand,
And heaven in a wild flower,
Hold infinity in the palm of your hand,
And eternity in an hour.

Many years ago when my laboratory began to make
headway into the study of cytoskeleton regulation in
yeast, I placed this stanza written by the English poet
William Blake (1757-1827) on the top of our lab webpage,
to illustrate our aspiration to crack a fundamental and
complex biological system by focusing on a specific
regulatory pathway inside a simple single-celled organism.
It has always been my belief that it is only possible to truly
understand the big picture after you have studied the fine
details. Now, light years away from science as a taxi driver,
I continue to believe that we can see a whale of a world in
a grain of sand.

And that is what this book is all about.

My arduous taxi driving career, of course, has been
anything but poetic. Nevertheless, the things I encountered
on the roads and the people I observed and interacted with
have made the endeavor more bearable and, occasionally,
even enjoyable. Though these experiences may seem as
trivial and incidental as any other ordinary thing you see or
do in your everyday life, I noted them down and presented
them publicly first in a blog, and now in the form of a book,
in the hope that these tiny "grains of sand" may serve as
seeds for thought for those who may find the stories
interesting and meaningful, and perhaps even nurture their
own opinions or perspectives on a grander scale.

My six months of taxi driving has certainly changed my own perspectives on life. I have learned many things on the roads as a cabdriver that I have never had a chance to learn before as a scientist. Now, I not only know so much more about the geographical and architectural layout of this country, but more importantly, I also came closer to the lives of the people calling it home. I became one of them. In this sense, I cherish this experience deeply.

Due to the recent expansion of the readership of my blog, several job opportunities have come up (for that, I am very grateful). It is now possible that my taxi driving career may have ended here. But no matter what I do in the future, the strength and wisdom I gained during these six months will remain with me for many years to come.

I also intend to carry my taxi driver's license for as long as possible.

About The Author

Mingjie Cai studied Biology at Nanjing University from 1973 to 1977. He obtained a Master of Science degree from the Shanghai Institute of Biochemistry, Chinese Academy of Sciences in 1981. Following several years of working at the same institute and later in the Department of Biochemistry at Nanjing University as a lecturer, he enrolled into the PhD program of the Department of Biochemistry at Stanford University in 1985 and obtained his PhD degree in 1990. From 1990 to 1992, he worked in the Department of Genetics at the University of Washington as a Damon Runyon-Walter Winchell Postdoctoral Fellow. He joined the Institute of Molecular and Cell Biology in Singapore in 1992 as a Principal Investigator. He had been an Associate Professor of the same institute and Adjunct Associate Professor in the Department of Biochemistry at the National University of Singapore from 2000. He also served on the Editorial Board of the International Journal of Biochemistry and Cell Biology (Elsevier, Amsterdam) from 2003. He was unemployed from May 2008 and became a taxi driver in Singapore in February 2009.

Appendix 1:

A Note On My Research Interests

Cytoskeletons, the skeletons of cells, are essential for cell survival. Unlike the human skeleton, however, cytoskeletons are made of simple building blocks such as actin, which can be assembled and disassembled rapidly upon stimulation. The cells need to assemble or disassemble cytoskeletons at various cellular locations in order to perform important functions such as change in cell shape, cell movement, or directed secretion or intake of substances. The rapid assembly and disassembly of cytoskeletons are strictly controlled by a complicated and poorly understood network of mechanisms which react to various internal and external cues. Abnormalities in cytoskeletons are found to be associated with numerous human diseases, such as neuronal disorders and cancers.

In more academic terms, we used a unicellular eukaryotic organism, Saccharomyces cerevisiae, or budding yeast, as a model system to study the mechanisms that control the dynamic of the actin cytoskeleton inside the cell. The yeast actin cytoskeletons are very similar to that of human cells not only mechanically, but also physiologically. The major actin cytoskeletal structures in yeast are the cortical patches and the cytoplasmic cables, both of which display cell cycle specific patterns of dynamics. Among a large number of proteins that have been identified to play important roles in the regulation of the actin cytoskeleton in yeast are a group of proteins that localize to the actin patches. Many of them are essential for structures and functions of the actin cytoskeleton and have conserved counterparts in mammalian cells.

In the past decade or so, the research from my laboratory had led to the identification of the actin patch-associated complex containing the proteins Pan1p/End3p/Sla1p/Scd5p, which is required for the actin cytoskeleton organization and integrity, membrane protein endocytosis, and cell wall synthesis. Moreover, my laboratory had discovered a novel family of protein kinases, including Prk1p and Ark1p, which modulate the activities of a large number of actin regulatory proteins including Pan1p, Sla1p, Scd5p, and Bni1p by phosphorylating them in a temporal- and spatial-specific manner, thereby affecting the patterns of the cytoskeleton assembly/disassembly.

The main focus of my research in recent years revolved around the molecular mechanisms of the regulation of actin dynamics and protein transport (endocytosis and exocytosis) by the phosphorylation of the Prk1 family of kinases.

Research publications:

1.) Mingjie Cai and Zaiping Li (1982). The organization of 5S rRNA genes in the silkworm Attacus ricini genome. **Genetics Sinica**, 9, 325-332.

2.) Mingjie Cai and Ronald W. Davis (1989). Purification of a yeast centromere binding protein that is able to distinguish single basepair mutations in its recognition site. **Mol. Cell. Biol.** 9, 2544-2550.

3.) Mingjie Cai and Ronald W. Davis (1990). Yeast centromere binding protein CBF1, of the Helix-Loop-

Helix protein family, is required for chromosome stability and methionine prototrophy. **Cell** 61, 437-446.

4.) Andreas Koerte, Terence Chong, Xiaorong Li, Kumud Wahane, and Mingjie Cai. (1995). Suppression of the yeast mutation rft1-1 by human p53. **J. Biol. Chem.** 270, 22556-22564.

5.) Hsin-Yao Tang and Mingjie Cai (1996). The EH domain-containing protein Pan1 is required for normal organization of the actin cytoskeleton in Saccharomyces cerevisiae. **Mol. Cell. Biol.** 16, 4897-4914

6.) Hsin-Yao Tang, Alan Munn and Mingjie Cai (1997). EH domain proteins Pan1p and End3p are components of a complex that plays a dual role in organization of the cortical actin cytoskeleton and endocytosis in Saccharomyces cerevisiae. **Mol. Cell. Biol.** 17, 4294-4304.

7.) Xiaorong Li and Mingjie Cai (1997). Inactivation of the cyclin-dependent kinase CDC28 abrogates cell cycle arrest induced by DNA damage and disassembly of mitotic spindles in Saccharomyces cerevisiae. **Mol. Cell. Biol.** 17, 2723-2734.

8.) Guisheng Zeng and Mingjie Cai. (1999). Regulation of the actin cytoskeleton organization in yeast by a novel serine/threonine kinase Prk1p. **J. Cell Biol.** 144, 71-82.

9.) Xiaorong Li and Mingjie Cai (1999). Recovery of the yeast cell cycle from heat shock-induced G1 arrest involves a positive regulation of G1 cyclin expression by the S-phase cyclin Clb5. **J. Biol. Chem.** 274, 24220-24231.

10.) Hsin-Yao Tang, Jing Xu, and Mingjie Cai (2000). Pan1p, End3p, and Sla1p, three yeast proteins required for normal cortical actin cytoskeleton organization, associate with each other and play essential roles in cell wall morphogenesis. **Mol. Cell. Biol.** 20, 12-25.

11.) Guisheng Zeng, Xianwen Yu, and Mingjie Cai (2001). Regulation of the yeast actin cytoskeleton-regulatory complex Pan1p/Sla1p/End3p by the serine/threonine kinase Prk1p. **Mol. Biol. Cell** 12, 3759-3773.

12.) Bo Huang, Guisheng Zeng, Alvin Y.J. Ng, and Mingjie Cai (2003). Identification of Novel Recognition Motifs and Regulatory Targets for the Yeast Actin-regulating Kinase Prk1p. **Mol. Biol. Cell.** 14, 4871-4884.

13.) Xianwen Yu and Mingjie Cai (2004). The yeast dynamin-related GTPase Vps1p functions in the organization of the actin cytoskeleton via interaction with Sla1p. **J. Cell Science.** 117, 3839-3853.

14.) Guisheng Zeng and Mingjie Cai (2005). Prk1p. **Int. J. Biochem. Cell Biol.** 37, 48-53.

15.) Bo Huang and Mingjie Cai (2007). Pan1p: the actin director of endocytosis in yeast. **Int. J. Biochem. Cell Biol.** 39, 1760-1764.

16.) Guisheng Zeng, Bo Huang, Suat Peng Neo, Junxia Wang, and Mingjie Cai (2007). Scd5p Mediates Phosphoregulation of Actin and Endocytosis by the Type 1 Phosphatase Glc7p in Yeast. **Mol. Biol. Cell.** 18, 4885-4898

17.) Mingji Jin and Mingjie Cai (2008). A novel function of Arp2p in mediating Prk1p-specific regulation of actin and endocytosis in yeast **Mol. Biol. Cell.** 19, 297-307.

18.) Wenjie Qiu, Suat Peng Neo, Xianwen Yu and Mingjie Cai (2008). A novel septin-associated protein, Syp1p, is required for normal cell cycle dependent septin cytoskeleton dynamics in yeast. **Genetics.** 180, 1445-1457.

19.) Bo Huang, Ling Ling Chua and Mingjie Cai (2009). Negative regulation of the actin-regulating kinase Prk1p by patch localization-induced autophosphorylation. **Traffic.** 10, 35-41.

20.) Junxia Wang, Suat Peng Neo, and Mingjie Cai (2009). Regulation of the yeast formin Bni1p by the actin-regulating kinase Prk1p. **Traffic.** 10, 528-535.

Appendix 2:

Expressways Mentioned In This Book

Pan Island Expressway (PIE)

The Pan Island Expressway (PIE) is the oldest and longest of Singapore's expressways. It extends along the length of the island, connecting Tuas in the west to Changi Airport in the east. It is 42.8km (26.6 miles) long.

East Coast Parkway (ECP)

The East Coast Parkway (ECP) runs along the southeastern coast of Singapore. The expressway is approximately 20km (12.4 miles) in length, and connects Changi Airport in the east to the Benjamin Sheares Bridge in the south of the main island before it links with the Ayer Rajah Expressway (AYE).

Ayer Rajah Expressway (AYE)

The Ayer Rajah Expressway (AYE) extends from the western end of the East Coast Parkway (ECP) in the south of Singapore to Tuas in the west near the Tuas Second Link to Malaysia. Together with the ECP, it forms a second east-west link to complement the Pan Island Expressway (PIE).

Central Expressway (CTE)

The Central Expressway (CTE) connects the city centre of Singapore with the northern residential parts of the island, including Toa Payoh, Bishan, and Ang Mo Kio. It is 15.8km (9.8 miles) long.

Tampines Expressway (TPE)

The Tampines Expressway (TPE) is a highway in the northeastern fringe of Singapore, joining the Pan Island Expressway (PIE) near Singapore Changi Airport in the east with the Central Expressway (CTE) and Seletar Expressway (SLE) in the north of the island. It is 14km (8.7 miles) long.

Kallang-Paya Lebar Expressway (KPE)

The Kallang-Paya Lebar Expressway (KPE) connects the East Coast Parkway (ECP) and the Tampines Expressway (TPE) in the northeast. The six lane expressway extends 12km (7.5 miles), with approximately 10km (6.2 miles) underground. It is the longest subterranean road tunnel in Southeast Asia.

Nicoll Highway

Nicoll Highway is a major arterial road in Singapore which links Kallang to the city. Despite what its name suggests, the speed limit on the highway is lower than that of an expressway, and it also has traffic lights at some of its intersections, which are not found on expressways.

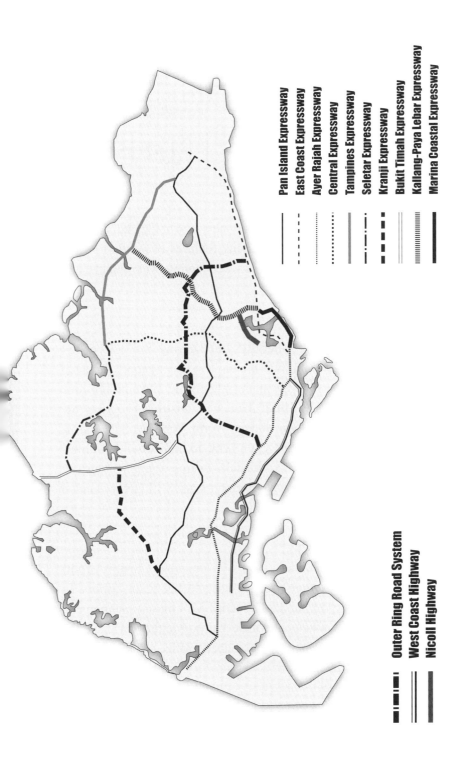

Pan Island Expressway
East Coast Expressway
Ayer Rajah Expressway
Central Expressway
Tampines Expressway
Seletar Expressway
Kranji Expressway
Bukit Timah Expressway
Kallang-Paya Lebar Expressway
Marina Coastal Expressway

Outer Ring Road System
West Coast Highway
Nicoll Highway

Appendix 3:

Noteworthy Places Mentioned In This Book

Ang Mo Kio

Ang Mo Kio is a heartland new town located north of central Singapore. It has many features of public housing neighborhoods including hawker centers, wet markets, and public housing blocks.

Bukit Timah

Bukit Timah Hill (literally "tin bearing hill") is a 164 meter (537 feet) tall hill, the highest in Singapore. Located near the centre of the main island, the surrounding area is also known as Bukit Timah or District 11. After the Japanese Occupation during World War Two, the farms and plantations there gave way to industrial buildings, and by the 1960s Bukit Timah became a major industrial centre. Today, these have been replaced with luxury landed property and condominiums.

Changi Airport

Located on the eastern edge of Singapore, Changi Airport is a major aviation hub in Asia and the main airport. In 2008 the airport handled a record 37.7 million passengers, making it the nineteenth busiest airport in the world and the fifth busiest in Asia by passenger traffic. As at 1 January 2009, Changi Airport is served by 83 airlines operating more than 4,670 weekly scheduled flights to 190 cities in 60 countries.

Chinatown

Chinatown is a neighborhood featuring Chinese cultural elements and a historically concentrated ethnic Chinese population. But as the Chinese form the largest ethnic group in Singapore, approximately 74% of the population, Chinatown is considerably less of an enclave than it once was. Chinatown is also known as *niu che shui* (牛车水), literally "bull-cart water", as its water supply was principally transported by animal-driven carts in the 1800s.

Clarke Quay

Clarke Quay is a riverside quay in Singapore, situated upstream from the mouth of the Singapore River and Boat Quay. Clarke Quay was named after Sir Andrew Clarke, Singapore's second Governor and Governor of the Straits Settlements from 1873 to 1875. Today, Clarke Quay is a vibrant entertainment area where blocks of restored warehouses house restaurants and nightclubs.

Geylang

Geylang, also known as Geylang Serai, is a neighborhood to the east of Singapore's central business district and the Singapore River. Conservation shophouses along Geylang Road are protected from redevelopment. Geylang is famous for its red-light district and good food, which create a distinctive atmosphere different from the rest of modern Singapore.

Jurong

Jurong, a town in the western part of Singapore, used to be a swamp until the 1960s when it was cleared. Jurong is split into two parts: Jurong East, a residential and commercial area, and Jurong West, mainly an industrial estate.

Jurong Island

Jurong Island is a man-made island located to the southwest of the main island of Singapore. Formed from the amalgamation of several offshore islands through land reclamation, Jurong Island today has an area of about 32km² (12.4 square miles) and is home to leading petrochemical companies.

Lau Pa Sat

Telok Ayer Market, also known colloquially as Lau Pa Sat ("old market"), is a building in Singapore's central business district. Gazetted as a national monument in 1973, Telok Ayer Market is currently a food centre, and has a unique Victorian octagonal cast-iron structure.

Orchard Road

Orchard Road is the retail hub of Singapore and a major tourist attraction. Often known simply as Orchard, it has an extensive underground pedestrian network linking many of the malls. Orchard Road got its name from the nutmeg, pepper and fruit orchards that were located there in the 1840s. Commercial development took off only in the 1970s.

Orchard Towers

Orchard Towers (also known as the "Four Floors of Whores") is a building located on the corner of Claymore Road and Orchard Road. The lower floors are a combination of bars and retail outlets where johns are supposedly able to meet and pick up prostitutes.

Outram

Outram is a district near to the central business district and contains the ethnic neighborhood of Chinatown. Outram Road was named in 1858 after a British general, Sir James Outram (1803-1863).

Queenstown

Developed by the Singapore Improvement Trust (SIT) in the 1950s and subsequently the Housing and Development Board (HDB) in the 1960s, Queenstown is the first satellite town in Singapore. Queenstown was named after Queen Elizabeth to mark her coronation in 1953.

Raffles Place

Located at the southern end of the main island, Raffles Place is Singapore's business and financial hub. It features some of the tallest buildings in the country, and is named after Sir Stamford Raffles, the founder of modern Singapore.

Shenton Way

Shenton Way is a major trunk road in Singapore's central business district, with skyscrapers flanking both sides of the road. Built almost entirely on reclaimed land, it was named after Sir Shenton Thomas, Governor of Straits Settlements from 1934 to 1942.

Tampines

Tampines is a large and densely populated residential area located in the eastern end of Singapore. Ironwood trees, or *tempinis*, once grew abundantly here and gave the area its name. The transformation of Tampines into a regional town began in the late 1970s, although it was not until the 1990s that the new town was fully established.

Toa Payoh

Toa Payoh is a neighborhood in the central region of Singapore, and is one of the earliest satellite public housing estates in Singapore. Toa Payoh means "big swamp" in the Hokkien language, referring to the large swampy area that preceded the later development of the area from 1964.

Thomson Road

Thomson Road is a major trunk road linking Singapore's central business district with the northern suburban areas. Its name comes from John Turnbull Thomson, who was the Government Surveyor and Chief Engineer of the Straits Settlements from 1841 to 1853.

Tiong Bahru

Built in the 1930s, Tiong Bahru Estate is one of the oldest housing estates in Singapore. It was the first project undertaken by the Singapore Improvement Trust (SIT), a government body administered by the British colonial authority to provide mass public housing in Singapore. The estate is a mix of art deco and local shophouse architecture.

Appendix 4:

Glossary

Electronic Road Pricing (ERP)

The ERP scheme is an electronic system of road pricing based on a pay-as-you-use principle. Adopted in 1998, Singapore was the first city in the world to implement an electronic toll road collection system with flexible pricing to control traffic congestion.

Housing Development Board (HDB)

The HDB is the statutory board of the Ministry of National Development responsible for public housing in Singapore. It is generally credited with clearing up the squatters and slums in Singapore in the 1960s, and resettling residents into low-cost government-built housing.

KL

Kuala Lumpur (often abbreviated colloquially as KL) is the capital of and largest city in Malaysia.

KTV

Literally, Karaoke Television. Usually refers to a Karaoke pub where hostesses are present.

Mass Rapid Transit (MRT)

The MRT forms the backbone of the railway system in Singapore and spans the entire island. The MRT has 70 stations with 119km (73.9 miles) of lines constructed by the Land Transport Authority (LTA), which allocates operating concessions to the profit-based corporations SMRT Corporation and SBS Transit.

Shophouse

A shophouse is an architectural building type commonly seen in urban Southeast Asia. Typically, shophouses consist of shops on the ground floor which open up to a public arcade, and which have residential accommodation upstairs. The shophouses usually abut each other to form rows.

Also published by Aktive Learning

The Student's Guide to Life is a must-have guidebook for twelve to twenty-plus year olds.

Inside they will learn how to:

★ Deal with emotional and self-esteem issues

★ Interact in a healthy way with parents, siblings and teachers

★ Make new friends and build lifelong friendships

★ Handle romantic relationships

★ Excel in school without studying all the time

★ Set goals, manage their time and achieve their dreams

"Gives great insight on the best ways to handle everyday tricky situations."
– Seventeen

"A useful guide for anyone dealing with the young." – Lifestyle

"Andrew pours candid yet practical advice to teenagers of all ages." – Teenage

---

The Student's Guide to Exam Success will help you maximize your grades with less studying, giving you more time to do whatever you want.

In this book you will learn to:

★ Succeed in school while having more free time

★ Score higher points in any type of question

★ Create a winning plan for tackling the exam

★ Study for the exam in the most efficient and effective way

★ Manage your time properly during the exam

★ Minimize careless mistakes and boost your score

"Andrew Tan shows he knows students all too well." - Lifestyle

"Can't understand how your schoolmates get to the top of the class? The Student's Guide to Exam Success has the answers!" - Teenage

Available at leading bookstores and online at www.aktive.com.sg